Black River Dreams

meditations on fly fishing

Black River Dreams

meditations on fly fishing

Maximilian Werner

hancock

house

ISBN-13: 978-0-88839-633-4 [trade paperback]
ISBN-13: 978-0-88839-443-9 [epub]

www.hancockhouse.com

Publisher: James D. Anker
Page design: Dutton & Sherman Design
Jacket design: Dutton & Sherman Design
Jacket photo: © Galyna Andrushko/Shutterstock
Author photo: Kim Werner
Frontispiece photo: Maximilian Werner

We acknowledge the financial support of the Government of Canada through the Canada Book Fund and the Canada Council for the Arts, and of the Province of British Columbia through the British Columbia Arts Council and the Book Publishing Tax Credit.

Hancock House gratefully acknowledges the Halkomelem Speaking Peoples whose unceded traditional territories our offices reside upon.

Published simultaneously in Canada and the United States by

HANCOCK HOUSE PUBLISHERS LTD.
19313 Zero Avenue, Surrey, B.C. Canada V3Z 9R9
#104-4550 Birch Bay-Lynden Rd, Blaine, WA, U.S.A. 98230-9436
(800) 938-1114 Fax (800) 983-2262
www.hancockhouse.com sales@hancockhouse.com

For Kim, Wilder, and Greer

Contents

Preface ix

Acknowledgments xiii

Part I
THE HAUNTING

Second Water 3

The Riverkeepers 13

The Dowsers of Perlite Pond 21

Black River Dreams 31

Part II

DEEP WATER

Angling at the Juncture of the Sun and Moon 45

The History of Ice 55

Coyote Grammar 65

Green River: A Memoir 71

Linear Drift: Reflections on Pacheta Lake 85

Part III

THE AFTERGLOW

Swan Song 99

Confessions of a Fly Fisher 107

Decision Water 117

The Killing Place 129

The Purist 139

Anglers' Ball 145

The Afterglow 155

Preface

Assuming we give our lives to what we love, fly fishing clearly ranks near the top of my list. In a good year, I probably spend 150 days on the water. And when I am not fly fishing, I do the next best thing: I write about fly fishing. Apart from the fact that I could not sit down and peck away at the keyboard for twelve hours straight, these two activities are fairly similar. They are work done joyfully. I'm sure there are many reasons—some shallow, some deep—for why this is, but in either case I get to celebrate the life I love. Of course the angling life encompasses a great deal and touches many subjects, but at the heart of this life are the places where trout live. I have lived in the West for almost thirty years, and during this time I have fished many lakes, streams, and rivers in Utah and Arizona. These are now my home waters. What is also true is that day calls to day and place calls to place when it comes to time spent on the water, which is why I have also included two pieces about fishing in Maine, where I spent the first eleven years of my life, and one piece about some freshwater fishing I did while visiting the island of Kauai. Sometimes the best way to appreciate one's home water is to leave it. Apart from these exceptions, these essays ponder western waters. But this isn't a guide book, at least not in the traditional sense.

How we feel about the watery earth and its creatures depends on our understanding. This understanding is very much like a drift boat that carries us down a great river. The river changes, but the boat remains unchanged much of the time. Usually our day-to-day lives flow by unbroken. But then, as we grow older, we run aground or float lazily through the shade of ancient trees and we are unsettled by the sublimity of life. We may then decide to change our lives. I think of Norman Maclean's little book *A River Runs through It*, which is an exquisite exposition of human fragility, natural beauty, and loss. Maclean shows us that most of our insights come through the contemplation and appreciation of small things: the smell of the leaves, the direction of the wind, and what is left unsaid between loved ones.

I, too, note the details: the stonefly husks, bird tracks, what strong wind does to water. I see how the auburn leaves curl and fill with light and shadow. And how, once fallen, they collect rain and temporarily fulfill the small creatures of the world. But I am not just a record keeper or a transcriber of the moment. I read the water, land, and sky and then reveal the weather in my head. As I later say in *Green River: A Memoir*, too often we take our stories to the river rather than from it. That is, for better or for worse, we impose our perspectives. The tendency to interpret the environment is universal, of course. Humans do it. Trout do it. Mayflies do it. Not in precisely the same way, but we all have to interpret our world in order to live in it. Over time, these interpretations become codified into stories, which are as basic to humans as facing upriver is to trout.

Fortunately, humans and other animals also enjoy some variation. For the trout this may mean eating a hatchling that has fallen into the water.

And what angler doesn't like to fish (or to read about fishing) new water from time to time? Occasionally, we want to be stunned by a new version of the riverine and cosmic story. This need for variety may help to explain how I can enjoy the mysticism I find in Maclean as much as I savor the biological realism I find in Hemingway. Obviously many writers—men and women both—have made significant contributions to a healthy and remarkably stratified body of fly fishing literature. I have singled out these writers because I identify with their differing visions, and because together they form the water that my book tends to inhabit.

I have arranged the essays roughly in the order they were written and grouped them into three parts. *Part I: The Haunting* consists of essays written at a time in my life when I was much more prone to mystical interpretations of the natural world. Under the spell of the inexplicable, I enjoyed a kind of numinous inebriation, as though of ethereal microbrew I had drunk and walked the moonlit banks, sight casting to the rising faces of the long dead and trout made of fog. It was a strange, happy, and anxious time.

After thirty-two years of inhabiting the self-stylized realm of my own subjectivity, I met a deep-sea fisherman and professor of American Literature by the name of Bert Bender. Shortly thereafter, I enrolled in Bert's *Ecology and 20th Century American Literature* course and experienced a kind of reverse religious conversion or enlightenment, as if I had been awakened, not to some celestial calling, but to the recognition of humanity's place within what Charles Darwin described as the community of common descent. As the study of the relationships between organisms and their interactions with their environment, ecology not only changed how I looked at myself, but also how I viewed other people and the many animals I encountered while on the water. Suddenly the activity of fly fishing had become an opportunity to speculate, wonder, and reflect on the seamlessness and grandeur of life. Ecology became an antidote to my mystic trance.

Although this change in perspective characterizes *Part II: Deep Water,* like the speaker of Theodore Roethke's poem "The Waking," I take my waking slow. I gradually began to appreciate the relational logic of life's complexity. I had, in effect, become a naked searcher. Instead of seeking alternative transcendental truths, I wondered how I fit into the natural scheme of things, together with the trout and the mayflies and whatever lives unseen beneath the water. Of all the things I discovered, the most important is that I belong to the Earth and to the water and was born of processes and according to natural laws to which every living thing is subject. This discovery was not necessarily a negation of mystical wonder, but it did make mystical interpretations seem a bit down the river. Thus, *Part III: The Afterglow* tends to embody this more realistic orientation to life.

However much this book may differ from other books, at the end of the day these are fly fishing stories. Alternately narrative, meditative, and lyrical, every one of these stories has fish in it. And sunlight, clean air, rain, and birdsong. And the grassy riverbanks and lakesides where I often sit in the prime of life, chewing a blade of sweet grass, watching the water and daydreaming and barely knowing the difference.

Acknowledgments

Thanks to all my fishing partners, past and present, especially Kim Werner, Nole Walkingshaw, and Jeff Metcalf.

I was fortunate to have a few people who were willing to read and comment on my work, but no one more so than my mother, Nancy Werner. I owe her a huge debt of gratitude for her readership and critical feedback.

No human being has had more of an effect on me than Bert Bender. I owe him my life.

I am deeply grateful to the biologist John Alcock for his willingness and ability to communicate complex ideas beautifully, simply, and directly; a skill he no doubt relied on when discussing biology with me. Whether those discussions took place while hiking in the Sonoran desert, or in the margins of this manuscript, John was always patient, supportive, and interested.

I also need to thank Professor Fred Dings. He knows why.

Many of these essays originally appeared in journals and magazines, including *Fly Rod and Reel, ISLE: Interdisciplinary Studies in Literature and Environment, Weber Studies: Voices and Viewpoints of the Contemporary West, Sporting Classics, Yale Anglers' Journal, The North American Review,* and *Fly Fishing Life Magazine.* I want to thank their editors. Special thanks to Jim Butler and *Fly Rod and Reel,* publisher of my first fly fishing essay.

Part I
THE HAUNTING

Late at night I hear the trees.
They're singing with the dead overhead.

—EDDIE VEDDER

Second Water

For Nancy, my mother and first water

When I was a kid, I thought that when I left a place the roots I had put down were cut. I now know some roots cannot ever be fully severed, and that wherever I have lived, I am still in some way there. At the moment, my roots are spread throughout the mountains and deserts of the West. But in the right light, I can see faint offshoots stretching east to Caribou, Maine, and to my childhood, where they undulate along the banks of Caribou Stream. I haven't set foot in Caribou since my family left in 1979. Not physically, anyway. I lie here in the high desert and wonder how the life I had then might have shaped the life I have now. However much it may seem otherwise, time is layered: it collapses, advances, and recedes. Among the layers, woven in the loam, are my dreams about Caribou. Perhaps they are trying to tell me something, but when I look inside those oblique proxies I do not find life, but rather the damp winding tunnels where life had once been.

Surely the past is a dissolving map, but I can still remember the day I caught and killed my first trout. Firsts are like other memories except their cores resist the fire of time and the aging brain. This explains why I can still see my neighbor Judy, a full-blooded Micmac Indian with a smooth brown face, full cheeks, and simple haircut. Judy was poor as dust, and though she had nothing, she would have given it to me if I had needed it. I recall her averted eyes as she gave me her father's old fishing rod. The rod—a six-footer with a spinning reel—was a going-away gift and maybe a little more. Within the week, my brother and I would say goodbye to Maine and to our father and then fly to Utah to join my mother and sister. Those days were some of the hardest I have lived, but Judy and angling for trout softened the strangeness of those hours.

I had never owned a fishing rod, so I could hardly resist going the moment Judy put the rod in my hand. I didn't, though, because I was well mannered and it was near dark. I asked Judy if her father didn't need the rod anymore, and she smiled. We both knew that wasn't the point, but I was disarmed by her kindness and in that state I resorted to foolishness. Then I felt embarrassed. Luckily, before I could say anything else, Judy's father called her inside. He had been sitting on the porch fixing a carburetor as the birds were bedding down and the last of the late spring light slipped over the house. Judy smiled at me and said *goodbye*. At nine years old, she was two years younger than me, but her spirit was as old as the Earth itself. She was very maternal, and with my own mother far away, I was grateful for her warmth.

Usually when I imagine my childhood self, I see him lying in the tall yellow grass or running along a stream through the woods for the simple pleasure of running. I'm more or less a detached observer. But sometimes he suddenly stops whatever he is doing and looks right at me, even though I am standing in front of a window in December, some thirty years down the road. *Why do you keep coming back here?* he asks. I think for a moment and I tell him I'm not sure. A sweet kid, his brow furrows and he nods, as if to reassure me that not knowing is as good as knowing. I put my arm around him in the half-light, and I don't know why, but then we search for answers in the black limbs of the oak trees.

Maybe all that is important is that my family and Judy's family shared this moment in the past the same way we shared the trees and the breezes that blew through them. June mornings still had a good chill on them, so when I awoke the next day I quickly pulled on clothes, grabbed the rod, and headed out of the shade, where I was happy to have the sun warm my back. The rod was sheathed in pinesap, and the reel seat fastener was gummed with fish blood. I flushed with excitement when I thought of all the fish the rod had landed and, I supposed, that it had once belonged to a great Micmac fisherman.

I considered leaving the rod as it was as a gesture of respect. But I also needed to make the rod mine, so I used some rubbing alcohol and cotton balls to clean it from top to bottom. Then I tied on what I realize now was probably a #12 leech. I had no idea the fly was a fly, nor that it was intended to be used with a fly rod. All I knew was that I had a strange hook with a clump of hair tied around it that had magically appeared on the windowsill of an otherwise empty house. My mother had been gone a week, but I could still see the squares of dust from where the boxes had been stacked on the porch. She had actually started packing a couple years ago, so she would often need the things she had packed—a pan, my sister's curling iron, a certain pair of shoes. She always found what she was look-ing for, but this went on until she unpacked half the boxes and had to start packing all over again.

I placed the alcohol and dirty cotton balls on the porch steps and noted the hole through which the resident skunk entered her den. A couple nights after my mother left for Utah, the skunk sprayed under our porch and the pungent odor covered everything within a thirty foot radius. After that, I wore a hat to bed, slept under three sheets, and put tomorrow's clothes in bread bags. At the time, it was the worst thing. But smelling like a skunk was the only justification I needed to quit school and spend my last days in Caribou wandering with the other animals. Incidentally, the one thing worse than a pissed off skunk is two pissed off skunks. But we learned to live with them like anything else: leeches, deep snow, ticks, wet mittens.

When Judy gave me the rod, it was as if she had given me the final word of a spell that, when spoken, would temporarily dissolve my troubles and find me angling in the mild June sun. Other than the Aroostook River, which was on the other side of town and therefore out of the question, Caribou Stream was the best place to fish for trout. As the outer boundary of my childhood stomping grounds, however, I had never gone to the stream alone. But now I was standing with that rod in my hand, the day getting older by the minute, and I had to make a choice: Go or stay put. Most of us get to that point in life where, if we want to do something, we either do it alone or sit and wish we had. I reached that point when I was about eight years old.

My inner map of Caribou has since faded, but I remember it rained in the night and the woods on the way to the trestle were thick with mist and mosquitoes. Somehow it seems strange to remember a rain storm that happened over a quarter century ago. A superstitious lot, the folks in Caribou would describe the storms as if they were the natural embodiments of various ill intentions: everything from *wicked*, to *confounded*, to simply *ill-mannered*. This was not one of those storms. It dropped a little rain and then left and was exceptional only in the sense that it was my last. And those were my last Maine mosquitoes; hovering, dipping, and waiting in the cool of the trees. I was wrong about some things as a kid, but one thing I knew for sure was that everything is hungry in the country.

As I neared the trestle I inspected the rod and line, which was clear and blue as a strand of my grandfather's hair. Though at the time he was not yet dead, I dreamed of fishing with my grandfather's ghost. I kept looking over at him, expecting him to say something, but we fished inwardly and without so much as a word between us. Then the sun went down and I didn't see him anymore. That was the only time he ever visited me in Maine. With our extended family content to remain out west, we were isolated. But isolation inspired us to make due. For me, that meant wandering, which I now did with the oldest purpose.

I got down on my hands and knees and then finally my belly and crawled the last ten feet to the trestle. The bank on the other side of the stream was a sunless, moody tangle of vegetation, but a few yards above the trestle, I spotted a small shoal of sand that signaled a feeder stream flowing out of the woods. Far below me, a few trout swayed. When I went for my rod, a rock slipped over the edge and the trout scattered. All but one black fish swam off. Then I realized it wasn't a fish at all, but that it was my face floating on the surface. I was a magical thinker as a child, partly because I *was* a child and partly because some places have that effect. Magic is not easy to understand, though. I think this is why I liked Judy so much: She was magic that could explain herself.

I remember standing with her on Farmham Stream, a small, silver thread of water that ran behind our houses. *Do you know that when the wind gusts in town it means the geese are leaving the lakes?* I put my hands in my pockets and fiddled with the dirt in the bottom of one of them. *Yes, doesn't everybody?* When the breeze rose in the trees, the sunlight lit Judy's face and I could see she was unconvinced. *OK, do you know water is my ancestor?* I played it safe and said, *No, I did not know that.* We took off our shoes and soaked our feet in the stream. She then said that after Micmac women brushed their hair, they would clean their combs and let the strands fall to the Earth, where they became rivers. *What about streams?* I asked her. Same thing, but the hair is children's. *Oh.* I liked that about Judy and her family: They were grounded by their magic, and their stories were like birds in that no matter how high they flew, they always came back to the Earth.

I crossed the trestle, stepped off the tracks, and studied the tall grass. The sun revealed a small path of oat-brown mud that I guessed led to the water. I held the rod shoulder-high and used my other hand to part the grass as I walked through it. Soon I could hear and then see the stream. The water was so clear I put my hand in it to make sure it was really there. Out of the corner of my eye, I saw a small dark flutter. A frog was looking at me from its perch atop a stone. I opened the bail and let the line slide across my fingertips as it uncoiled into the water. A few seconds later I reeled up the seam. The fly swam just beneath the surface, and I enjoyed how well it imitated the fluid wiggle of a leech. Then the water suddenly thickened into a trout that charged out from the bank and seized the fly.

The fish's ferocity caught me off guard. I was unprepared for the tugging and thrashing, for the violence of an animal fighting for its life. This was not what I had imagined. I wanted to let go, to be done with it. The trout pulled farther and farther down stream. Perhaps it was because of this distance that I finally mustered the presence of mind to lift the rod tip and finish what I had started. By then, the trout had taken about fifteen feet of line, which is considerable in a stream that size. I doubted the trout was still there, but I reeled and reeled and brought the trout to hand. In my excitement, I squeezed the trout so hard his eyes bulged. I turned to tell someone who was not there that I had caught a fish. The sun was burning a white hole through the trees. Emboldened, I told the trout his luck had run out. As I worked the hook from his mouth, he stiffened and silver bubbles rose from deep inside him and I am almost certain he said that I would also take a turn.

Thus the trout was still very much alive, and I needed to get some place where I could change that. So I bagged him and headed for the house. I took the shortcut over two fences, then up Farmham stream to the cemetery, where I stood atop the falling stone wall and mapped the way I would take. At that age, there were reasons not to dilly-dally in the cemetery. The older kids would go out there with beer and candles and hold séances. Other times they would use the Ouija board, and that would have gone on indefinitely had the doctor's daughter not asked the-one-question-you-do-not-ask and died when the board said she would. I was young, but I remember those stories as well as the roughness of the stones, the drizzles of gnats, and the names severed by shadow. I did not dare step on the headstones lest the unkind dead spoil my dreams.

Midway through, I came to a grave and startled a cat and her nursing kittens. I thought maybe they smelled the fish because all they did was hiss and twitch their noses. Covered with matted hair, the mama cat looked awful and I told her so. She watched me until the trout curled like a tongue in my bag. *You're hungry, aren't you girl?* I figured this was as good a place as any to clean the trout. I judged the hour and knelt in the damp grass. The earth was soft and my knees soaked the rain and stung until I couldn't feel them. I had not killed with my hands and part of me couldn't believe I could do what I was about to do.

I slipped my buck knife from its sheath and wiped the leaves from the stone, which recorded a single day on Earth. I might have brooded on that for a long while had not the largest kitten of the litter stolen my attention by catching a cricket and eating it, song and all. I slid my hand down the trout and eased him from the bag. Although my fingers were pink and clumsy with cold, this time around I tried to be careful, which seems odd, considering. Just as I feared, the trout had fight left in him. I turned him over and cracked his head lightly on a stone a couple of times. As if I were not quite killing him. Didn't take much, fortunately. By the mama cat's definition, I must have been taking a long time because she looked at me and yawned.

Beyond the cemetery, someone tried and tried to start a chain saw. A porch door slammed. I slid the knife vent to gill, just as I had seen my grandfather do on the Snake River. *Look there,* he would say, lightly pressing on the swim bladder with the tip of his knife. *See that? That's the spirit sack. Always open it.* I poked a small hole and the bladder deflated. My eyes watered into my mouth. I didn't mind sipping my eye water, but I had to see, so I wiped my eyes with the tops of my wrists. Then I lifted the bundle of organs and tossed it to the cats. Not quite weaned, the kittens acted confused. Mama cat purred and growled as she ate, her green eyes soft and half-shut, then crazed and wide and wild. The trout felt light in my hand, like an envelope from which a letter had been taken.

When I got to my yard, I saw Judy and her father working in their garden. It was evening and the treetops were noisy with crows. I looked down at my bag and when I looked up again I saw Judy and her father resting on their tools, watching me. Judy put down her hoe and walked out to meet me. She stood close and looked into the bag. *Brook trout.* Her breath smelled like the pine needle that hung from her mouth. *I'll cook it,* she offered. As we walked toward her house, I asked her what was worse than being born and dying on the same day. *Nothing,* she said. *I figured you'd say that.*

Judy's father was already standing at the sink, washing his hands and looking out the window. The room was dark, but a nice fire burned in the potbelly stove. He looked at me and then at Judy. Then he said something in Micmac, and Judy responded and pointed to my bag. He nodded, smiled, and held out his hand. *He'll cook,* she said. I sat at the table in a soft wool blanket, listening to fish, potato, and yellow onion in the pan. I wanted to say thank you but instead I wrapped my hands around a mug of warm milk, breathed the heat of pine, and tried to let go.

I wondered how it would feel to close the door of our house for the last time and about all the *lasts* to follow. Before we left, I would walk to Judy's house and return the rod. It didn't seem right to take it from that place, and I could not imagine needing it where I was going because I could not imagine where I was going. After that, I would take my last ride down

Sweden Street and over the Aroostook River and its silent roiling, then on up the hill and out of town without once thinking to look back. I cannot remember my father's last words before we boarded the plane that would carry us west, but I know he said them and that it was not easy.

Judy stoked the fire as I finished up the trout. Light from the stove flickered across the bone comb on my plate and a black and white photograph of Judy's great grandmother. I could see night building and decided I would not move until I saw my father's headlights or the light go on in my brother's room. As I sat in that chair, one by one, my favorite haunts came and went. I said goodbye to the lakes and to the woods and, of course, to Caribou Stream.

Then I thought about our land outside of town and how I would miss it. Each fall my father, brother, and I would rise before the sun and travel an hour north and spend two days clearing some twenty acres of grass and brush with a sweeping wall of fire. My father set and spread the fire while my brother and I made a game of running and leaping through the flames. Sometimes the wind picked up and on it I could smell the coming snow. The newly fed fire would rise until I could not see my father and brother. Just as suddenly, they would reappear behind the flames and the hot ash would swirl and swirl around them like disintegrating stars.

When the burning was done, we would walk across that monotony of ash toward our camp in the white birch trees. There my father would smoke his pipe and look ahead to next year's burning. The last time we burned, though, he didn't talk about next year or any year after that. But the years were still there, unspoken, underground, a mesh of moist, white roots searching, widening, and rising toward the charred mice that could not reach their holes; and thus the knowledge that things can be and still not be, and that if I do not get right with the places I leave, they will always feel like fires from which I cannot run fast enough.

The Riverkeepers

Fifteen years later

F all has come and shawls of frost hang in the windows. I wipe my eyes and look outside and see a small wind bothering the copper-green leaves of the maple trees across the street. I think I hear my nose whistling and so I hold my breath until I realize the sound is coming from a crack in the window. I put my finger over the spot and it stops. Patches of stars shine through a thin haze of clouds and the old moon, eyeballing me and yellowed from wood smoke and the smelters of Kennecott Copper Mine, is about to sink into Salt Lake. I look over at the clock as I pull on my longjohns and grab a sweater, which has filled the room with the sweet, dry smell of wool and cedar chips. The crack in the window goes from a whistle to a hum. I recognize the tune: It is the song cold makes, and I sing it only when I am warm. As I watch a light go on in a house up the street, I wonder about the first people to inhabit this valley, and what cold must have looked like to them.

Later, I try to explain this curiosity to my friends as we drive up Parley's Canyon toward the North Fork of the Duchesne River. Nole's driving, I'm riding shotgun, and Tae is in the back seat, cupping a mug of coffee. I've known these guys for half my life, and this affords us a certain luxury: We do not worry about interpreting each other's silence. Nole's a "towhead," and as he nods, his white shock of hair undulates back and forth like stocks of smoke, or the *ghosts* of hair. It's dark in the car, but I can still see his sharp profile. "Deer," he says, gesturing toward a pair of doe on the side of the road. Then he honks a few times until they startle back up the mountain. I look back at Tae. He smiles his upside down smile. His glasses are fogged with steam from the coffee. "It's all good, bro," he says, reaching forward and clutching my shoulder. I lean back and watch the sky fade from bruise-purple to flamingo-pink.

We soon reach Currant Creek Junction, the last town before the river. "We need anything?" Nole asks. "I'm good." Tae looks at me, "I need a dance partner." A few minutes later we begin climbing toward Wolf Creek Pass. We drive through pine and aspen, which from afar look like they've been set on fire. I crank down the window and suck in the wet, pine-sweet air. When I pull my head back in the car, my face is sanguine, numb and damp with early morning mist. Nole smiles at me. "Feel better?" "Yeah," I say, "baptism by air."

Tae is inspecting his flies the way a jeweler inspects his stones. "What are they taking up here?" I ask him. "These," he says, "and these." He holds two nymphs in the light, one in each hand. "Looks good. Buggy. I'd eat 'em if I were a fish." But then the river comes into view. Nole turns off the music and we all get quiet. Without the sun shining on it, the river looks dark and deep. "Flows look good," Nole says as we cross a small, single-lane bridge. We turn down a little dirt road and take it right to the river. Nole parks in a stand of large cottonwoods, so smooth and white they resemble the tusks of elephants. The air is heavy with the smell of soil and a part of me wants to lie down on the river's edge and sleep, not because I'm tired, but because sleep seems the best way to *be* here, to fully immerse myself in the place.

From time to time the sun—that supreme articulator—comes out and turns the water to a pale, blue-green. I close my eyes and lift my face to warm it. When I open them again, I see Nole and Tae sharing a run twenty yards upriver. As Tae rolls his line forward into a riffle, and I watch the loop of it glide across the water like cursive, I am reminded of why I sometimes refer to him as *Bruce Lee with a fly rod*.

After a moment I hear a splash. Nole has one on. "What did he take?" I holler. "WD," he calls back excitedly. Then the trout erupts from the water, arcing side to side in an effort to throw the hook. "Nice little bow," Tae says. I nod. Even from this distance, the trout appears sharp and bright like a plump shard of steel, strange and deliciously out of context. A couple of minutes later, Nole gently holds the trout in the shallows. He tilts it back and forth like a mirror to catch the sun, admiring its hues of silver and carmine. Then it's gone.

"There he is," Tae says, setting the hook as his daisy-yellow indicator dips out of sight. I stand tiptoed to glimpse the fish, "Looks like a thirteen incher." Tae starts to reel in line that's floating at his feet like a bunch of green scribbles. "Brown?" he asks. "Yeah," I say, "that or a bow." He guffaws, "Doesn't feel like a bow. Too stubborn." The fish swims toward us, sees us, then bolts to the center of the river. "Definitely a brown." "Yup," I say, "but go easy. No need to saddle up."

Tae loosens his drag and then slowly works the trout into a foot of water. He asks me to get his camera. "I want to get an underwater picture." He points to his backpack. Then, holding his rod tip up with one hand, he submerses the camera, points and shoots. I look upriver and see Nole working the inside line of a nice run. Tae sees it too. "Get up there and get you some of that," he says, brushing away a leaf and a few blades of grass to reveal the trout's stippled markings. "I'll flex on him after I water the bushes."

I plant my rod between two large stones and walk off river into the thick pines. Once inside, away from the running and lapping of the water, I hear the trill of a bird I look for but cannot see. The forest floor is spongy and slick with pine needles. I look around to make sure I'm alone. I smile at my absurdity. "The woods are lovely, dark and deep," I whisper, and like a soliloquy to no one or to the trees I recite as much as I remember of Frost's poem. The syllables melting on my tongue like flakes of snow. I look up and that's when I see a large, red squirrel watching me from a pine branch a few feet away. The moment he sees that I see him, he sounds what seems to be both an alarm and a scolding. A few seconds later I hear another squirrel. Then another. I smile. "All right," I say, "I'll go."

I find Tae and Nole lounging on some rocks a few yards upriver, sharing a tin of sardines and some crackers and enjoying the warmth of the October sun. "How did you do?" I ask Nole. He hands me a cracker with a chunk of sardine on it. "Caught four. All bows." I put down my rod and take a seat between him and Tae. "You're the golden boy. What about you Doc Fu?" "Landed three, lost three," Tae says, matter-of-factly. I take a pull off of my flask and pass it around. "Got your hare's ass kicked, did you?" He looks at me cross-eyed and I laugh. Across the river the trees go dark and ignite again as a cloud passes over the sun. "There's one," Nole says, pointing to a flash in the center of the river.

"He looks nice. Get on it, boss." "All right, Doc. Don't mind if I do." I free my fly from where I've hooked it on a ferule and walk toward the river. "Don't spook him," Nole says. As I near the river, I hunch down and eventually kneel on the water's edge. Once there, I strip out some line and roll it a couple yards above the trout. I watch my strike indicator drift over his head. Nothing. I cast to him twice more. Not even a flutter. "It's probably some idiot's beer bottle," Nole says. "No . . . it's a trout. I'm going to check him out."

When I get within a yard of him, I'm sure he's going to bolt but he doesn't. I lean down until my face is just above the water. The North Fork is clear and cold, and as I peer down into it I see why the trout—a fourteen-inch bow with beet-red gills as thin and delicate as crepe paper—did not take my fly. "He's wedged himself between two rocks," I say, incredulous. I roll up my sleeves and watch the trout undulate with the approach of my hand. I slide my fingers beneath his belly and then, with my thumb just behind his pectoral fin, I slowly ease him back, freeing him. I weave my fingers together and cradle him for a few moments while he rests. Then he swims off.

We spend the morning fishing our way deep into the Ouray Indian Reservation. A dense blanket of clouds has drifted down from the north, and while it's only midafternoon, it looks and feels like evening. A cold drizzle has begun to fall, turning the gray stones black, but the air *smells* like snow. My eyes are blurry with cold. I pull on my rainwear as a dipper skitters along the river's edge, alternately calling and sipping water from the shallows. Around the next bend I see riffles, slow water running beneath a cliff, a headwater pocked with boulders. I look back at Tae and Nole, who are lunching just inside the tree line. Nole's got his glasses off so I can see his ice-blue eyes. With his lean build and blue-gray raincoat, he looks like a blue heron. "I'm going to walk up," I say. As I turn to go, I hear "Think fast." When I turn around, I see a red apple in the air above me. I catch it. "Ah," I say dramatically, "the forbidden fruit. Can't pass that up." Nole smiles, "Didn't think so."

As I near the cliff, I puzzle over the color of the water, which has changed from a clear, pale green to a milky blue. But when I reach the pool I know why: A band of sulfur forms the cliff's base, and it has been seeping into the water. A caddis fly alights on the bill of my cap, walks down my cheek, and flies away. Then, on the pool's seam of slow and rushing water, I see the dark head of a rising trout. I sink to my knees and switch to a caddis imitation that I invented, a fly I call *The Deputy.* I rub some floatant on the fly's hackle and abdomen, strip out some line, and then cast just inside the seam, where the water's surface is silky and scalloped. Startled by a pair of warblers, I lose sight of my fly until a silver-dollar-size hole opens in the river and sucks it in with a splash.

The poet Wallace Stevens once wrote, "I do not know which to prefer . . . the blackbird whistling or just after." Against the blue froth of the water, my leader is a shade away from invisible, and as it slowly cuts through the film, and I feel the veins in my neck grow heavy with blood, I can't help but think of my own, albeit halting version of Stevens's line. *I do not know which to prefer, the moment before a trout strikes, the moment it strikes, or just after.* The trout swims to the bottom of the hole and stays there. I use the moment to look around. The rain has stopped. To the east the sky has turned to the blue-black tones of evening, but the west, still gauzy with cloud, is pumpkin orange and match-head red.

I feel the trout begin to swim up the seam, slowly at first, then in a rush. He runs about three yards and then rises into six inches of water. A rainbow. After I reel in my line, I raise my rod tip straight up—twelve o'clock, one o'clock, two o'clock—until the trout glides into my hand. Flecks of dusk pepper its deep blue back and trickle down its aqua green sides, a slash of phosphoric red, the lateral band burning, paling to glare-ice white. By now Tae and Nole are standing over me. "A beauty," Tae says. I slip the fly from the bow's lip and point it toward the center of the river. Even after the trout has dissolved into the chalky blue water, we stand there, lingering, our breath coming out our mouths like the auguries of our ghosts.

Minutes away from dark, we decide to cut up through the pines to a dirt road instead of walking the river. I see gold swathes of sawgrass and beaver streams that glow like mercury in the gloaming. Nole spots a fox, a red tail. We stop and watch it slip through the grass, its bushy tail blazing. Now that we are still, we can hear the whir of gnats and mosquitoes. "Supper time," I say, and that is all it takes to get us walking.

Strange how darkness changes a place, I think as we drive the winding road toward the pass. I hear the *tink tink tink* of moths hitting the headlights. A few seconds ahead of us, a deer—eyes shining—jumps in and out of the road in one motion, its shoulder muscles rolling under its skin like waves of water. *Strange how such vastness can be reduced to what you can see in your headlights . . . and how this exclusion teaches me to see more intensely.* As I look at Tae and Nole, and realize that each of them is gazing at a world that may be different from the world I see, I want to tell them what I'm thinking. But I don't. I listen for the night's sounds, knowing that being here is enough.

A week later I'm home looking at the pictures from our trip. When I come to Tae's underwater picture of the brown he caught, I take pause: I am struck by how *present* the trout looks, by how beautifully adapted it seems to what I imagine must be its surreal existence. But then, as my eyes float up from the fish through the cold, greenish blue water, I see the unmistakable face of a man, an Ouray Indian. While no bigger than a dime, his face—his brow, nose, cheekbones, and slightly opened mouth— is remarkably distinctive. And he appears to be looking down from a great height, as if into an abyss.

When I look at his face now, I mostly feel a sense of calm and reverence, as though his residing in that river somehow meant that it would be protected. I don't know if I can ever fully explain this feeling, this spiritual heaviness, but I come close when I imagine the obliteration of time or a connection to a *living* history; an awareness that is borne of a species' successes and failures, pleasures and pains, gods and devils. So when I look at Tae or Nole, or that exquisite rainbow on the end of my line, I experience millions of years of persistence, the realization that I am both the *many* and the *one* who keeps—and is kept by—the river.

The Dowsers
of Perlite Pond

For Hartford

*Time is not a straight line, it's more of a labyrinth, and if you press
close to the wall at the right place you can hear the hurrying steps
and the voices, you can hear yourself walking past there on the
other side.*

—Thomas Transtromer

*I think that the star
glittering above me
has been dead for a million years.*

—Rainer Maria Rilke

I think twice before calling Perlite Pond a home water if only because
there is a small town of folks who live within walking distance of it.
I know this relationship doesn't entirely make sense, but still I figure the
pond is more theirs than mine in an ecological sort of way. More mine
than someone's from anywhere but here. In capitalist terms, however,

Harborlite Mining Corporation owns the place and does what it wants, which is mine perlite and, therefore, keep non-mining related activities to a minimum. But animals depend on their water holes, and therefore it seems unnatural that we be kept from them. I also know animals succumb to the will of animals, that lions typically defer to elephants. I decided to drive out to the pond today because today it's raining and I like to mine the moods of the rain. The last time I saw the place was two years ago, and part of me has been worrying about it ever since. As I travel east on Superstition Freeway, I realize that if all the streets were gone I could still find my way: This time of year the moon splits Gonzales Pass and so leaps from the cliffs of Apache Leap, over town, and then rises directly above the pond. Because of the lunar blues of the ground and cliffs and water, I like to think the moon rises *out* of the pond, too.

Unless I discover a secret place, my awareness of it is a gift, and the giver usually belongs to the place as much as any characteristic of the place itself, be it the fish or water or sky. And so as I'm driving toward the pond I think *Chris Hartford*, although I could also call him *knot of worm wood, dump truck, gummed wicker, Castenada's thesis,* or just plain old *money you don't recognize.* When we got to Arizona, my wife Kim and I rented a sixty-year-old adobe house on the corner of Mill Avenue. The dining room was decrepit and encased with swinging windows, and a wheel on the wall was once used to roll away the roof and thereby replace it with night and moon and starlight. The original owner, a Hungarian immigrant who also designed the home, had painted a beautiful but now defunct panorama of the Superstition, McDowell, and Camelback Mountains on the ceiling. Fifty years later, some bored tenant would add the yellow mushroom cloud of an atomic bomb.

Chris was our landlord's senior handyman, even though he was not even thirty at the time. I was out in the yard the day we met, staring at the first pomegranate tree I'd ever seen, and listening to unfamiliar and dusky birds whistle in the tangle. He had come to hang a door he had made. Symbolically, I figured that made him an already significant human being. I asked him if those rattling birds were some kind of crow and, later, whether the landlord was hiring. He said the birds were grackles and hell yes he was hiring. Wilt was always hiring. Wilt was a hoarder and we regularly drove truckloads of his collectibles seventy miles from Tempe to a gutted nightclub in Superior. Actually he had caches all over Arizona, but at the time I worked for him, the nightclub—which was also used as a church at one time and contained row upon row of huge iron shelves—had not yet reached capacity. In other words, we still had a little room to walk and could see much of the ceiling.

Scorpions were new and terrifying then and I felt a stirring when I'd see them hanging like freakish earrings in the webs of black widows. Some webs looked like tooled smoke floating between the aisles of furniture. Others reminded me of those crude rope webs in mutant spider horror movies. I took my lighter and burned the anchor strands at their bases and watched them drop away. I then carried the airy body of a stuffed horned owl with a baby skunk in its talons to the belly of the building. The shelves there held dozens of such birds and the mounted heads of mammals, including a bull and cow elk, a whitetail deer, a North American bison, a black bear, a mountain lion, and two antelope. The collection also included a massive timber wolf that I considered the leader. He had one bald and broken ear and looked old and oddly celestial with his star-white face and albino eyes.

Chris walked by and said he was going for a swim at the pond, his face brown with dust and a beard of shredded wheat. His hair was a few months short of accepting a ponytail, but that didn't stop him. We drove by his place and picked up Blue. Blue was basically a yellow Lab-Chow mix that was so big around it looked like he was wearing a barrel under his skin. Therefore, his lumpy head looked ridiculously small, and so did his ears, and his brow was broad as an anvil and deeply furrowed. Together, the aspects of his face did not create an easily decipherable mood. I know it sounds contradictory, but I'd have to say he looked *knowingly bewildered*, especially when panting. And except for its very edges, his tongue was blue as deep water.

Thousands of miles away, the melancholy and milky glow of the sinking sun withdrew as we drove out of town. We had turned and headed south along a washboard mining road when we came to four old cottonwoods and a small creek. Chris slowed as we neared them but still as many turkey vultures with their roasted heads dropped from the treetops and flew out of sight. Chris and I sat side by side, but Blue, who was too fat to sit, stood over me and hung his head out the window. He obviously knew where we were going because the closer we got, the more he whined and grunted. For reasons I did not fully understand, Chris did not believe in "chopping a dog's nuts." Therefore Blue still had his balls, and when they were not swinging dangerously between his legs, they were swinging between mine. A couple of minutes into Blue's whining session, Chris explained that the pond was unnatural and occurred when miners blasted into a spring that coursed some eighty feet beneath the earth's surface. Not the most readily assimilated fact given my essentially noninvasive approach to nature.

We parked in the shadow of a boulder and took a thin path down to the water. Many animals used the path and their tracks dimpled the sun-dried mud. We passed through another small group of cottonwoods whose pale green leaves sounded like Bible paper when the breeze picked up. Blue was already in the water and Chris was quick to kick off his work boots and join him. I sat on the bank and took off my shirt, shoes, and socks. A volcanic glass, perlite is sharp, white, and flaky as frost. I slid my palms lightly over the ground. As I did so, I noticed dark bits of obsidian. Around here they're known as Apache Tears and the locals sell them for five dollars a bucket.

Once the water settled, several small bass appeared in the shallows, fluttering above nests of sand. An aqua-silver color, the fish looked like they were cut from tin. I put my feet in the water and the largest of the bass—a six or seven incher—swam over to inspect my toes as I wiggled them. By now Chris and Blue had swum to the other side of the pond and were sitting together in the water. They were both about the same color so it took me an instant to determine who was who. I could hear the electric whir of gnats in the tall grass along the shoreline. The gnats were so small, I glimpsed them only by looking past them, which is the same way I glimpse fine rain. Somewhere behind me a red-wing blackbird sang a song made of water. I wanted to see it so I walked toward the sound. As I neared a patch of cattails, the hidden bird stopped singing. *Not who you had in mind?* I thought, remembering that the song was not for me. I decided to focus on what *was* there, instead of on what was not. Deep as the water was, I could still see the flare-ups of sunfish floating in an old sedan on the pond floor.

Blue barked two sharp barks. I looked up and saw another dog across the pond walking quickly toward me. He had his nose to the ground and I hoped it was Blue he was after. Then a man walked out of the trees with a shotgun and I realized it didn't matter. Chris saw him too and started walking back too slowly along the pond's edge. I went to my shoes and looked down shore for the gun. And then for the man who was carrying it. When he saw Blue, the man called *Cinnamon* to his dog and got her to heel. He was thin and shirtless with white hair on his head and body, and his eyes looked very bright and swollen, as if they had leather bags of wine beneath them.

When somebody has a shotgun on one side and a dog on the other, it's hard to know if he's reasonable, but Chris took Blue by the hackle and greeted the man and the three of us got to talking. The man said the day was a hot son-of-a-bitch and that he was out here watching over the place. He pointed at the water and said a boy had drowned just last week while diving for obsidian. The boy was drunk and the man said he guessed that might make dying a little easier but that anyway people in town were mad as hell and folks over at the mine didn't want anyone out here. Neither Chris nor I knew what to say to that so we nodded dumbly and then looked at the dogs.

Pretty soon the three of us were laughing as Blue, whining and porcine, chased Cinnamon in circles. The old man commented on Blue's *skinny-ass-legs*, and wondered if he didn't have some poodle in him. I figured the man had a fondness for poodles because then he said we could swim if we kept it to weekends so as to avoid the blasting and we left it at that. Driving back later that evening, Chris and I saw two boys and a brush fire burning toward town. Chris pulled off the road and watched them. He said he wanted to be sure they got where they were going.

At the bottom of every dream, there is a pond. Ponds are the floors of dreams. I dreamt I was standing in the dark, silky water. I held a net several yards over the pond and tried to catch copper-green fish as they leapt for dragonflies. In the dream, I understood these dragonflies were made of moon and I remember watching them closely. Each time a fish would jump, I saw my face reflected in its side. We all had the same dark eyes. Then the fish started turning into children and I woke up. Sometimes I'll dream of a friend I haven't seen in years and I'll wake feeling like I ought to check on him. Not even two months had passed since I last saw the pond, but upon waking from my dream of it, I felt a similar urgency. That summer, my wife's younger brother, James, was visiting from Utah, and in an effort to rescue him from another day of television, air conditioning, and Pepsi-Cola, I asked if he wanted to drive out to a pond. Do some swimming. He sprang off the couch like a rubber band and said a herd of wild horses couldn't keep him from it.

Since it was Saturday, I expected to see other cars or at least a riot of bikes when we neared the pond but didn't. We descended a small hill into the leafy shadows of a lone cottonwood tree. I was anxious to fish for bluegill before the sun got high, but James looked at me and said, "Lead this horse to water." Despite his zeal, I was swimming before he had his socks off. The water was warm at my armpits and cold below my waist. I dove three feet to the cold and opened my eyes and saw bits of silt and murk. As I emerged, I exhaled long and slow, as though I had gone down a great depth. James's skin looked sugar white in the glare and he had his arms folded across his chest: "How deep's that water?" "About thirty," I said. The soles of his feet looked very pink and soft, and he minced down the bank as if he had never gone barefoot. Once in the water, he cocked his head like a snake and mapped his route. He looked a little wild. After he had swum a few feet, he treaded and said *ah* and that the water was real warm. I considered revealing he was treading in about the same place a boy had drowned. Then the thought occurred to me: If spirits exist, there can be no such thing as privacy.

Chris Hartford once told me that those warm pockets of water were the souls of animals. But I didn't tell James that either. I left him lying in the sun and I walked back to the truck to rig up. From there the pond looked cloud-white where the sun fell on it. I scanned the cliffs and thought I'd work their shadows. When I got to the pond's edge, I glimpsed the flash of a lure rocketing over the water. A boy of about twelve was spinning in the shallows of the pond's eastern end. I passed him on my way to the cliffs and we nodded and said *hello* when he checked his cast. He had a milk jug of water and a tackle box that overflowed with bright minnow patterns, day-glo jars, line, and bait hooks. A nice largemouth bass was clipped to a stringer. I worked my way down shore and rounded the pond, where I expected to see the caretaker's trailer but saw only a few broken cinder blocks. A pair of coots, their bills curved and white as the ends of Swisher sweet cigars, startled and looked back at me as they swam away. By now James had been seduced by obsidian and he puttered along the banks with his eyes to the ground. *Time to fish*, I said. Beneath the cliffs, the pond deepened rapidly, leaving only a few white boulders that made me think of half-finished sculptures and elephant skulls in moonlight.

I took a huge step to the first boulder, steadied myself, then rolled my bugs into the water. As I waited for them to sink, I watched the boy. With the cliffs behind me, I envied the ease with which he cast and the possibilities of his water. He was jigging a portly gold worm over the weed beds and talking to himself in Spanish. Then his rod tip bowed and bounced tight. Once he had the fish on the stringer, he cast again and then yelled to me, saying the fishing was good there, and that if I wanted I could fish across from him on the other side. *Thank you*, I shouted back, raising a hand in a kind of salute, *I'd at least like to look at those fish*. He started reeling in and by the time I got to him he was holding a copper and rubber jig in the sunlight. *Do you have anything like this?* I said I didn't, that I was using flies. I felt foolish but grateful that he didn't seem to mind my foolishness.

I told him my name and asked for his. He looked at me, nodded, then turned and cast. *Armando*, he said. I heard his line hit the bail as his bait sailed across the pond and landed on the other shore. As if he were fishing a mouse pattern, he popped the jig into a few inches of water and then began pulling and flitting it above the weed beds. The lure was a good fifteen yards away, but the water was so clear and still I could see a large bass just as it slammed the lure. At first the fish came easily. Then it must have seen us or the bass on the stringer or both because it turned so hard and fast that it snapped the line.

I was expecting Armando to cuss or show frustration, but he merely looked at me through his bangs of dark hair and smiled. *I caught the same fish yesterday*. Figuring he had left another lure in the bass's mouth, I asked how he knew. He picked up the milk jug and drank deeply. *He's only got one eye . . . want some?* he said, offering me the jug. I told him *thanks*, but that I was going to try the pond's upper end and maybe I'd see him around. He knelt on the pond's edge and looked back and forth between the water and his tackle box until deciding on a lure. When I got to the upper end of the pond, I looked back. Armando had another fish, and as he fought it, his pole bent and dipped, as if it were a divining rod and he were a dowser of fish.

I met James back at the truck a short while later. He asked me how I did and I called him *old two-tone* because half of his milk white skin was sunburn red. His pockets bulged with Apache Tears. As I began tearing down my rod and packing up, an old primer-gray Chevy pickup passed us, trailing a curtain of dust. A young woman drove and a boy rode across from her with his arm out the window. I glanced at James and immediately suggested he put on a shirt, sit in the truck, and drink some water while he waited for the fires on his skin to start. He looked at his chest and arms, *Looks like I got bitch-slapped by the sun.* Then Armando and his family pulled up. He sat out his window and held up his stringer of bass. *Do you want these?* he asked. *They're very good. You're not going to eat them?* I asked, stupidly. *No, you can have them,* he assured me, his voice so kind and cleansing, it seemed on the verge of becoming water.

I do. I like to mine the moods of the rain and memories of my days on the water. Today I've practically got to walk a spell to reach the pond because Harborlite has strung boulders across the road. That's fine, keep out the truck. The rain is cold and steady. The ground is soft. Everything smells like rain. When I get there, the pond is not dead. It is strong and dark and its shores are clear. *This is the last time I'll come here*, I tell myself. I won't worry about this pond anymore. I've found a place where I can keep it all. I feel like I should be whispering. Like I should be praying. Then I remember the timber wolf standing in the dark of years ago. I see him there. Soon he takes a few steps and shakes the dust from his coat. Then he looks back at me. Those pale eyes glittering and persisting like stars.

Black River Dreams

For Bert Bender, the mere professor

Somewhere out ahead of me
a black bear sits alone
on his hillside . . .

—GALWAY KINNELL

Doused with smoky sunlight and evening shivers, an Apache stands on the Black River. When I gaze at him, I see a man grown from rich soil, night whispers, shadows, sharp air, and the inexplicable rustling of leaves. His young face and bare shoulders evoke stones smoothed by water. Behind him, the fleshy greens of grass, vines, and cottonwood leaves soften and clarify the lines of his body; the long lean arms, pale as the skin of sycamore running into rills of sand; his legs a pair of mountain streams. Judging by the weight and angle of the light, it is just before dark in midsummer, a few years shy of one century ago. But then Edward Curtis took many of his North American Indian photographs at twilight, perhaps to imply a subject on the brink of vanishing.

Though I feel like I still have one foot on the Black River as it was in 1904, I return to the moment when my wife, Kim, points out a large bird perched on the last lamp to light the Superstition Freeway before it empties into the desert. I duck to get a look. My knowledge of birds is burgeoning, and I can see it is a red-tailed hawk. When we pass under him, I ask Kim if she can see a dark band around the bird's belly. I want to be sure I'm correctly naming what I'm seeing. She rolls down the window and out goes her shadowy blonde hair. After a quick study, she says it does, that the band looks like bits of black cloth separated by fissures of down. Once we leave the freeway and begin driving southeast toward Florence Junction, signs of civilization appear less and less, until only the occasional headlights from passing cars and roadside crosses adorned with bright plastic flowers ignite the dying darkness.

I glance at the hills to the south of Gonzalez Pass, which were razed by fire a few years ago. The mountains didn't get much snow this year, but this elevation got enough rain to grow a light haze of grass around scorched barrel cactus, prickly pear, and the still-standing corpses of century plants. Like wondering at the calm, blue-eyed face of the billboard-Jesus in Superior, or at the ever-changing and otherworldly slag heaps farther up the road in Miami-Globe, checking the hills has become a ritual of travel. And yet each time I pass by here, I am struck by how long the desert takes to heal from fire.

My reverie is interrupted when a cottontail rabbit hops into the road and begins nibbling on a tuft of grass. His long ears glowing pink in the dawn. Out of the corner of my eye, I see Kim looking at me, her lips slightly gathered and on the verge of words. I'm pretty sure I know what she's thinking as I ease off the gas and grip the wheel. Ten years ago we were driving to Lake Powell to do some camping. We had gotten a late start and were about fifty miles from Bullfrog Marina when the sun went down. In that part of the desert there are good reasons not to drive at night; among them the narrow and winding road, and the many animals—real and imagined—that suddenly appear in it, such as coyotes, cows, owls, snakes, lizards, mice, and dozens of rabbits.

Most of the time we did not have a problem. The rabbits would just race alongside us in a game or in terror and then peel off into the night. Once or twice, though, I nearly wrecked trying to avoid a couple of smart asses who cut *across* the road instead of away from it. Kim is calm as water on a windless day, but nearly wrecking scared her so much she insisted I *hit* the rabbit instead of risking a crash. For the next few miles, I did not see one animal and thus was not confronted with implementing her solution. We could see the glow of lights rising into the sky as we ascended the last hill before Bullfrog Marina. At the summit, the road broke right, and no sooner had we come out of the turn when an enormous black-tailed jackrabbit appeared in the middle of the road.

He rose up as if to get a better look at us, and I remember thinking he looked oddly purposeful standing there. I had once seen a martial artist on television almost leap a speeding car. I say *almost* because the man broke every bone in his foot when it caught the top of the windshield. Still, he came close and he was not even built for jumping. Why not the rabbit? Then again, what if he is really in an ecstatic stupor? I thought about swerving, but the sting of Kim's scolding was still burning my cheeks, and so even though I probably had time to safely avoid him, I didn't. After the rabbit disappeared under the car with a thud, I looked at Kim and could see that she was troubled. But I felt afraid. Partly for superstitious reasons. Partly for reasons I cannot explain.

That was ten years ago. At this moment, however, I don't have to make any decisions I might later question: By the time we get to within fifty feet of the rabbit, he finishes his meal and, supremely camouflaged, vanishes the instant he enters the desert. I look at Kim to see how she's feeling. I have looked at her face nearly every day now for over a decade. Read and studied it. I like to think I have gotten better at understanding what it means. Sometimes it is still difficult, but just as often her eyes and hair and mouth fill with the growing light of spring and it is easy.

Not long after Globe, we enter the San Carlos Apache Reservation and the town of Peridot, the last place to get gas before the Black River, which runs some eighty miles to the northeast and serves as the border between the San Carlos and White Mountain Apache Reservations. As we wait for the clerk, Kim and I are joined by two Apache men who place a case of beer on the counter. I look at their dark vermilion hands and the broken moons of earth beneath their nails. Their sleeves are down and buttoned. I smile and nod. Their faces shine like buffed leather. "Breakfast," one says, then laughs. We all smile. As we pull away, I watch them in my rearview mirror. The wind billows in their shirts. Their teeth flash as they walk through the early morning dust, across the deserted railroad tracks, down their own well-worn paths of war.

A few miles later, we leave the highway and head north into prairie and cattle country. The wind barrels down off the Nantanes Plateau two thousand feet above us, whipping up brush and hurling grasshoppers into the windshield, splashing it with their vivid and beautiful deaths. In the distance, a coyote trots across the cropped and copper-colored grass. She regards us once or twice, but at no time does she stop along this place of danger. I once talked to a young Mescalero who came from San Carlos, and he told me his people walked this very road to the reservation when it was created in 1871.

Knowing what I do about the history of the Apache, I never feel at peace when I travel out here. I feel something mysterious and inscrutable, like the sensations before a lightning storm, when the air tingles, and it feels like something final is about to happen. I try not to take these feelings personally. Such an approach doesn't work: Something always ends up maimed, degraded, dead, or extinct. But the impersonal approach is also dangerous and perverse: In its extreme form, it is the impetus for hacking off the hands of mountain gorillas and using them for ashtrays.

Ahead I see what look like small black stones in the road, but as I near them they suddenly break into slashing and reckless flight. If not for their calls, which sound like the whistle of burning wood, these birds—Juncos, perhaps?—would pass for leaves. I wonder why they would gather in the road when they have such vast landscape to rove. I hesitate to think of a road as something that *supports* animal life, yet clearly its pitted surface not only traps seeds and insects that blow across it, it also makes them easier to find. There must be more to this explanation, I remind myself. And yet wondering is what carries me, however far, into the experience of being here.

I roll down the windows and the truck floods with the light, piquant smell of wet pine and rain that is falling to the north. Just before our ascent into one of the largest stands of old growth ponderosa pine in the world, we pass a finger-painted sign for the Slaughter Mountain Ranch. Words look so strange out here, on *this* page. I can see a mile or so down the road, but still there is no sign of the ranch, and I begin to think it is actually a mythological place where ghosts roll in red dust and don new bodies. On the horizon, the storm drifts like a dark curtain, and lightning bolts fracture the black sky. Within moments, we gain two thousand feet of elevation and enter a forest of pine and fir, which soon tapers into lush meadow and grassland laced with horses and wildflowers.

Where forest and grassland meet is Point of Pines. Place names are rarely so immediate and literal, except in Indian country. For without the spattering of crouched houses with their sagging roofs and wood piles, a small herd of Appaloosas, and a life-size cutout of Smoky the Bear leaning on a shovel, a point of pines is almost all there would be. The silence and stillness, coupled with a sign that reads "Caution: Low Flying Aircraft," suffuse the place with a Roswellian sense of the forbidden. The sign had fallen into the grass and flowers, where the words looked unfamiliar. The wind dies down and we hear the songs of crickets as we head up country on a rutted two-track road. The longer we listen, and the deeper we go, the less our need for words becomes.

We are quiet for a long time, but I break the silence when I see a pair of bounding pronghorn. Against a background of yellow grass and low-lying clouds, the two look faint as blowing dust. I admire their ability to resist definition. The huge ravens picking their way along the road are another matter. Whether by virtue of their regal strut or their sheer size, ravens command notice. Somehow when I look at them I think of creatures wearing raven *costumes*. Once we have passed, and it might seem we are no longer watching, I half expect them to lift off their headpieces and shed their plumed bodies. Maybe that is why I have sometimes seen their flattened and ragged husks in the road like wrecked kites.

Waterholes are scarce out here, so the few we pass are usually inhabited by bevies of cows and their offspring. While the adults give us a perfunctory glance and then return to ruminating, the young do not take their eyes off of us, least of all when we pull over to get out and stretch. Farther out, on the periphery of the waterhole, small groups of yearlings swagger in the building heat, their tails swishing wildly. Just beyond them, alone and outstretched in the grass, I see what appears to be one of their dead. Then another, and another, until I have counted eight dead cows, all within fifty yards of the waterhole.

Kim and I take hands and walk out to investigate. We walk wide of the yearlings, but still the largest of them stands and bawls at our approach. I have learned to be mindful around cows ever since one chased me and my dog through the woods along the Provo River in Utah. She was not satisfied until we were deep in the middle of the river. But young males are not much of a threat, so once I am sure he is not going to charge out after us, I attend to the fallen animal at my feet. *Cows don't really look like cows without their heads,* Kim says, keeping her distance. I kneel down for a closer look, for the story this ruin might tell.

Instead of a massive skull, a stump of spine projects from the shoulders, and the cow's sunken hide falls over its bones like a sheet over a piece of broken furniture. We wander from cow to cow and find them all headless. I think back to a trip my friend Nole and I took one late winter to the Strawberry River, when we had spotted a decapitated animal on the side of the road. The animal was so large, from afar we thought it was a horse. But once we got right up on it, we realized we were seeing a twelve-hundred-pound bull elk.

In the context of a remote canyon road in eastern Utah, the question, "Why would someone chop off a bull elk's head?" would seem to contain its own answer. After all, big bull heads grow big bull "trophy" antlers. But in the context of the San Carlos Apache Reservation, why someone would chop off a cow's head is not self-evident. By now, Kim has wandered out to look at another cow. In the vastness of wind-swept grass and deep blue sky, she appears small and distant, and the longer I watch her, the more it seems like she has swum far out into deep water. *Let's get going,* I call to her, careful to hide my nervousness. Then I look down the road and scan the horizon, knowing full well whatever is bothering me cannot be seen.

As we descend a series of switchbacks toward White Crossing, Kim glimpses the river through a band of pines and sycamores that have grown very tall so as to reach the sun. After a couple of last turns, the road steepens and straightens, and it is then that we see another sign. I admit that sometimes whether or not I pay attention to a sign is partly determined by the condition of the sign itself. I am thinking of one bent and rusty *No Trespassing* sign obscured by willows on a certain stretch of the Weber River in Utah, and of how—through some circuitous and inane mental process—I concluded that the sign's disrepair meant that whoever posted it must not *really* care anymore if I fished on his land. But *this* sign, although weatherworn and riddled with bullet holes, had an undeniable message: WARNING—BEARS IN THE AREA.

We are both eager to get out and explore, so we drive only a short distance before selecting a campsite. We park beneath a trio of ancient pines whose trunks I cannot quite join my arms around. The shadows smell cool and leafy, and for a while we just stand there, breathing. Then we walk down to the river. As we near the water, fleeing crawdads churn the shallows and a night heron calls out once. I look far upriver and slowly work my way back, looking for places where trout—and bears—might hold: I see a rise form in the slow water, a jam of pale logs, a riffle, and trees dark enough to hide us all twice.

After we set up camp, Kim and I rig up and walk to the riffle. I do not see any rises or bugs on the water, so I tie on a trusty bead-head hare's ear and soft hackle pheasant tail tandem. I clip on a weight and pay out line until I have enough to cover my half of the run. This is Kim's first season fishing rivers, and though she is remarkably patient and present when she fishes, I watch her for a minute or two to make sure she does not need anything. When I see that she has made a fly selection, I roll my bugs into the edge of the current and begin mending my line. Within a couple of minutes, I have caught and released a muscular, twelve-inch rainbow. Kim looks over at me and I shrug.

Normally when I catch a trout on the first cast, I take it to be a sign that the fishing is going to be productive. But after an hour of casting and several rig changes, neither Kim nor I had hooked up. *The new river blues*, I thought. Then I saw that Kim's scalp was pink with sun and suggested we sit in the shade and eat some lunch. The night heron we had seen earlier was back now, hunting minnows in a small pool across the river. Every now and then, a crow flapped its wings and cawed from some hidden perch high on the cliffs, but other than that the day was hot and still, except for the river, but even it seemed to toss in its own aquatic sleep.

After we ate, Kim and I walked upriver and found a nice riffle that graduated into a long section of flat water. I spotted a couple of juvenile smallmouth bass lolling just off shore and remembered hearing that the Black's bass population was so numerous at one time that fly fishermen were flown in by helicopter to thin them out. I did not know if the story were true, or if I even liked it, but before I got a chance to think about it, Kim called *Come check this out*. When I got to her, she was running her fingers so delicately across the trunk of a scrub oak, it was as if she were touching a wound. And I guess she really was, in a manner of speaking, because there, in the trunk, were four deep slashes.

The next time I run into a philosopher, I intend to ask him how I could have recognized something I had never seen before. But since they were *claw marks*, perhaps the question would be better put to an evolutionary psychologist. The marks appeared to have been made some time ago, but Kim and I were compelled to look around and listen. The shadow of a large bird flew upriver. A cricket sang and petered, sang and petered. Then I glimpsed the bear, but he was very far away, on a hillside in my head.

Because of its higher elevations and colder water temperatures, the upper Black is said to offer better trout fishing, so on a return trip a few months later, Kim and I decided to drive upriver to the Ten O' Diamonds Ranch area. To get there, we had to drive ten miles east of White Crossing and then descend a thin mountain road, and so it was not until late morning that we finally reached the river. A handful of ruddy steers were lounging along the banks in the shade, and as we neared them the largest rose and led the others spiraling quietly into the trees. Once they had gone, I walked a short distance to the river and watched it course down a jumble of black rocks into a mellow pool whose seams swirled with sun-whitened sticks, last autumn's leaves, and the moony heads of rising trout.

After we made camp, I tied on a caddis fly imitation and waded across the river, hopeful that the hatch was still on. The water was cold and clear and alive with bubbles. *The trout here must be happy*, I thought, recalling the day I first realized trout *could* be happy. I was fishing the confluence of the Salt and Verde Rivers one morning when a tanker-truck drove in and backed up to the river. I had not seen one other angler all morning, but the moment the truck appeared, a dozen spin-fishermen sporting coolers and fold-up chairs poured out of their waiting places and positioned themselves along the river.

The driver of the truck got out and lowered a section of pipe until it hung a few feet above the water. I looked at the fishermen and many had their bails open and arms cocked in anticipation of the first cast. The driver pulled a lever, and out burst one thousand gallons of water and rainbow trout. They hung in a cloud of water before hitting the river, and I could see many of their faces and perpetually wide-open eyes. The moment they entered the river, hundreds of them rose up on their tails like trained dolphins and skittered atop the water. The morning sunlight fell into their mouths, and they swam it down into the dark pools where the worms were drowning.

Kim called to me from the truck and asked if I needed anything, and I replied that I needed her to fish. Below me, the river shallowed and lightened into a gray-green and spilled through an array of boulders that reminded me of beehives. Then the river curved and pressed against the bank, where it ran very black and sexy through the thick, white roots of a giant cottonwood tree. Though tight, the run was prime, so I understood when a big trout broke its glassy surface. Kim was rigged for nymphing, so once she had made it down the bank and had crossed the river, I suggested she work the pool while I dry-flyed farther down. We turned on our Walkie-Talkies because we would soon be out of sight and hearing. I watched Kim fish for a couple of minutes and then made my way to the feeding trout.

The stretch was well protected by branches, but a short ways downriver I found a door. After a couple of botched casts, I placed the fly in the opening and began slowly mending line. When the strike did not come, I glanced upriver and saw the very tip of Kim's rod, but she was obscured by distance and branches. I was preparing to cast again when she called me on her radio. In a calm yet urgent voice she wondered if a bear were in our camp because the truck was rocking. I asked her if she were sure it was not a cow and she said not entirely, but she *was* sure she had heard sounds that a cow would not make. My mouth became very dry, and I quickly waded out to a boulder in the middle of the river.

I stood up on the boulder and looked toward the truck, which was parked some fifty yards away. For an instant, I thought I saw a bear sitting in our camp, but I was so far away, and there were so many shadows, I could not be sure. Still, having never encountered a bear in the wild before, my heart leapt at the thought and I radioed Kim and told her to reel in and start walking toward me. Apparently, my alarm was well concealed because she had not even finished reeling in by the time I had reached her. *I don't know,* she said, *it was probably a cow. It's been quiet up there for a while.* We were only twenty yards away, but from where we stood, we could see only the very top of the truck. I still had the shadowy bear in my mind, so I put down my rod and waded across the river to investigate.

When I reached the top of the bank, I did not see a bear sitting in our camp. I saw the torn screens of my camper top windows, and then a black mass in the back of my truck. Naturally I turned right back around, slid down the bank, waded across the river and told Kim I was fairly sure there was a bear in the back of the truck. *We have to do deal with this,* I said, matter-of-factly. Kim's face was flushed, excited and vaguely haunted, and for an instant I thought she was wearing a mask. *What are we going to do?* she asked. I told her I didn't know, and without thinking I drew my knife and slowly waded back across the river and up the bank. There he was: the bear that drags campers from their tents, who fishes alongside fishermen, and who does not in the least resemble Smoky.

In reality, the bear was sitting quietly, almost Indian-style, with our canvas bag of food in front of him, eating. I could see him all and he was very beautiful, but I could not think to admire him. Now my knife felt very small and my hand wanted a spear, if only to keep the bear at bay should it come to that. Kim was a few feet behind me, and her nearness incited me to yell, "Go away, bear!" I must have found the right combination of sounds because I had not said the words three times when the bear took the bag of food in his mouth and disappeared up the hill into the trees.

That night I lay awake for a long time. When I closed my eyes, I heard the river and saw my fly riding on top of it. Over and over. I could hear breezes in the woods and down in the rocks. Fainter still, turkeys gobbling and the long, high screams of elk. Then Kim said something and added her own night noise. Dew had settled all around us, and I could feel her hot breath on my neck. *What?* I whispered. Silence. *She is dreaming*, I thought. I rested my ear just outside her mouth and listened a few moments longer. When she did not speak, I pulled the blankets over her shoulders. Then I wondered at the dense cover of stars. At all the eyes gazing out of the cold and sheltering dark.

Part II
DEEP WATER

Nor will I know what voice spoke through my sleep.
I know only that there are simple powers, strange and real.

—Linda Hogan

Angling at the Juncture of the Sun and Moon

I

At a time when many Americans were boarding ships and crossing the Atlantic for the first time, someone asked Henry David Thoreau if he himself had traveled much. A cultured man, Thoreau replied that he had . . . throughout Concord. I remember his response because of its wit, of course, but also because it suggests a person can spend a lifetime becoming intimate with his residence, his place of dwelling, his own back yard. I think this is what most of us mean when we talk about our local fishing holes, that particular stretch of river or ocean, pond or lake where we spend our days learning the water and the life it makes possible. I have been fishing Christmas Tree Lake for four years and think of it as a home water (aren't all waters?), but I recognize there is still much to know about the lake and one of its most elegant residents, *Oncorhynchus apache*, the apache trout. What it means to know a place, or another creature, however, is a question I could answer for a lifetime.

In June of 1999, my friend Nole and I made our first trip to Christmas Tree. Nole lives in Salt Lake, where he has access to any number of world-class waters, but it did not take much convincing to get him down here: All I had to do was describe what promised to be an exceptional fly fishing experience. At roughly 8,500 feet, the lake occupies forty-one acres in the heart of the Mount Baldy Wilderness Area in the White Mountains of eastern Arizona, and the White Mountain Apache Indian Community manages it as a sport fishery. At that time, the lake hosted a considerable brown trout population, but since then the tribe has increased bag limits for browns in an effort to establish an exclusively apache trout fishery. Apart from a few other lakes in the area, Christmas Tree is the only place in the world where anglers can catch this beautiful, native fish.

Before coming to Arizona, I lived in Salt Lake, too. I could fish three excellent rivers in one day if I had wished, so initially I was disheartened when I learned that Arizona's best trout waters are nearly four hours from my home. Later, however, I would come to cherish the travel, and to regard it as an opportunity to reflect. Perhaps fly fishing is so uniquely fulfilling because the rudiments of travel—the lulls and the highs—serve as a counterpoint to the reward of destination. In fact, I don't see how a person can ever really know a place until he appreciates how he got there. This is especially true when traveling to Christmas Tree Lake, or to any lake in the White Mountains. Although it is possible to get there by way of Payson, I like to take the Superstition Freeway east toward the awe-inspiring Salt River Canyon. When Nole and I passed through there in late June, the sun was hanging just overhead and its light fell into the river, where it cooled into a deep blue-green. When I see that color again, I will probably be dreaming.

I am fairly certain that beauty is painful because of our seldom realized—and often misunderstood—need to possess it. But daydreaming drivers beware: The Salt River Canyon is not the place to lose one's self in reverie. Unlike so many of the environments I find myself in presently, this landscape commands one's complete presence. As Nole and I descended into the canyon, we saw a wrecked car a few thousand yards below the road on the other side. *Every canyon has one*, I thought. Years later I would meet a young Mescalero Indian man whose father died in the canyon when the semi he was driving left the road. He was hauling thirty head of cattle when it happened. That was the only conversation I had with him, and yet I cannot drive here without thinking about him, his father, and those cows.

Notwithstanding the immediate need to be mindful each time I drive it, the canyon always helps me gain perspective about what matters: space, clean air, water and soil, sun and shade, the awareness that we truly and deeply need places like this. Thoreau didn't consider himself much of a fisherman, but he did haunt the waters and wander the woods of his hometown, and by doing so he came to understand that we must value and protect the health of the natural systems on which life depends.

Not long after climbing out of the canyon, we reached Carrizo Junction and then headed south-southeast toward the small town of White River. This two-lane stretch of road crosses upland country distinguished by its rust-red soil and rich array of yucca and cacti. The light is soft this time of year, and the land looks hazy against the hard blue sky. Webs of red dust swirl across the road. I felt a little sleepy so I rolled down the window and devoured the cool air. I looked over at Nole and he had done the same, except his eyes were closed and he was smiling. I thought, *Why are you smiling, Walkingshaw?* But I didn't ask because I already knew.

If lakes were judged with the same ranking system as rivers, Christmas Tree Lake would qualify as a *blue ribbon* fishery, but without the crowds. By making a few wise management decisions, the Apaches can offer exceptional fly fishing in a relatively pristine environment. In addition to patrolling the area regularly, the White Mountain Apache tribe does not permit camping on the lake. Although many anglers rent rooms in town during the colder months, I prefer to camp at Hawley Lake, which is about ten miles north of Christmas Tree. There's a small general store there that sells domestic beer, soda, hot dogs, chips, coffee, and any number of ready-made food items. The store also sells maps, lures, line, permits, and firewood. The walls of the store's entryway are covered with hundreds of pictures of people admiring, holding, kissing, dangling, and generally disrespecting trout they had caught at Hawley, which is basically the "come an' get 'em," put-and-take, catch-and-kill lake of the White Mountains.

One picture, taken on a sunny autumn day in 1996, shows a boy of about ten holding a rotund, four-and-a-half-pound brown. The trout is so large, the boy must hold him up with both hands, his small, pink fingers all but disappearing in the trout's golden folds of hard-earned belly fat. The boy is thin and he is wearing an oversized ball cap with a tipped up bill, and for a moment I imagine the trout suddenly becoming aware of his own strength, at which point he leaps out of the boy's hands, smacks him with a pectoral fin, and lifts the boy over his head. What strikes me most, however, is that the boy appears to be crying. But why?

A host of possible answers comes to mind. But knowing what I do about children, I decide that the boy has never seen anything as beautiful as the fish he is holding, and that he is crying because whoever is taking the picture will not allow him to return the trout to its home. Then again, it is also possible that someone—perhaps a friend who is not pictured—farted on the boy's bologna sandwich and that is why he is crying. In any case, the pictures tell a story about our attitudes toward nonhuman nature. Maybe the key to having a responsible relationship with the world is to wonder what these photographs (or our actions) will mean at least a century from now. Will they make us smile then?

We drove out of town on Route 55. After a mile or two, the road parallels the east fork of the White River, and from that point on I slowed and we marveled at a greenery of shimmering cottonwoods, lush grasses, and hearty junipers. When the sun hit just right, the river flared through the trees and the mayflies glowed. A horse swished its tail in a field of turned earth. I realized I was daydreaming when Nole asked, "What's that?" and pointed to something lying in the road. I hunched over the wheel for a better look. "Oh, shit," I said, "it's a dog." I steered wide of him and slowed to a stop in the shade of an old cottonwood tree. No sooner had Nole rolled down the window, the dog lifted its head, stretched, barked once sleepily, and then laid his head down again.

Soon the road turned to dirt and we headed north into the mountains on Route 30. Rain was falling a mile or so to the east, and by the time we reached the lake it had already drenched the place and moved on. The trunks of giant ponderosa pines steamed as drops of water fell from their branches. The wet soil and mountain flora smelled delicious, and the cool mountain air filled my lungs like a tonic. The lake is shaped like a horseshoe and we rigged up and put in on its northeastern shore, not far from Moon Creek, which is one of two creeks that feeds the lake for part of the year. The other, Sun Creek, also flows out of the east but drains into the southern tip of the lake. As I kicked out into the water for the first time, scanning for rising trout, I remember liking the idea of fishing at the juncture of Sun and Moon Creeks. *What do you fish for there?* I imagined someone asking. *Do you dress your lines with cosmic dust? Do you bait your hooks with stars?*

II

The closer I sleep to water, the heavier my dreams become. A stream with frozen shallows ran through a band of pines. The sun was out, and the snow beyond the trees was blinding. A wolf walked out of the trees with her tail up and her muzzle was flecked with red snow. Before I could feel afraid, she sat next to me and we watched an impossibly beautiful trout swim beneath the ice. The wolf breathed slow and deep, and I could smell the wildness of the elk in her stomach. I felt hungry, and soon that hunger woke me. I looked outside and in the early June light I saw our camp was furry with frost. I knew Kim would want a fire so I slipped out of bed, dressed, and stepped out into the cold. Once I got the fire going, I put the water on for coffee and watched as the sun turned the frost to dew. Fires and reflection go hand in hand, and as I warmed my hands and drank my coffee, I recalled a trip Kim and I had taken a couple of years ago to a lake near Hawley.

We were fishing our way back to the put in, and as we neared shore, we saw two men preparing to fish the evening hatches of winged ants and blue-winged olive mayflies. The water was so riddled with circles, for a moment I thought it was raining. But then I looked closer and saw the emerging insects and the bobbing heads of feeding fry. I could hear the men talking and they were wondering if they had just seen a wolf on the edge of the woods. If they had seen a wolf, it was a Mexican Gray, a member of a pack that was reintroduced to this area by the Apaches not long ago.

The sun had fallen into the trees, and as we drove back to camp that night, I thought about another wolf that had been killed by a car a few miles west of Flagstaff. She had left her small group in search of a mate. Instead she found the strange, dying world of human progress, a world that had not seen her kind in that area since 1976, when the last wild Mexican Gray was reportedly shot. But I have confidence in the tribe, and an enlightened public, to nurture and protect the wolves. At one time the Apache trout was living an equally precarious existence, and although the restoration of the fish has had its challenges, particularly with regard to maintaining the species' genetic diversity, this exquisite fish has been nursed back from near extinction.

A cold, rain-sweetened wind blew out of the north and down my neck. I was here with Nole a little less than a year ago, and I am struck by the difference in temperature a few weeks makes. That trip fell on a weekend, but today is Monday, and I have yet to hear a human voice. Nole and I did all right by some definitions: Combined, we connected with about twenty-five trout—all browns—over the course of two days. But clearly we did not understand the place, its habits and rhythms, its cycles of feeding and repose.

After recollecting that trip in the context of a little research, I realized Nole and I had caught the tail end of the blue damsel hatch, an event that is comparable to the salmon fly hatch on the Yellowstone River, or the cicada hatch on the Green. This time, however, I knew better, and I therefore timed our trip to correspond to the appearance of the damsels. Kim would be awake soon, so I took the moment to peruse my flies and tie up some tandems, mostly Stimulators and Elk Hair Caddis with Peacock Lady droppers. A favorite for Christmas Tree, the Peacock Lady imitates the damsel's nymph stage, and it is as beautiful as its name.

I would later learn how easy it is to tie the fly, but on my trip with Kim I stopped at Hon-Dah Ski & Outdoor Sport in the town of Hon-Dah and bought a dozen of them from a young Apache man named Virgil. Virgil runs the place with another man by the name of Richard, and between the two of them, we get everything we need to fish Christmas Tree, or any other water in the White Mountains. I'm not sure if Richard fishes, but Virgil does, and he usually knows what is fishing well and what is not. How he conveys this information, however, is another matter. Whenever I think of Virgil I am reminded of Coyote, the creative and mischievous deity in North American Indian Mythology.

Coyote is a notorious trickster known to both help and hinder humans, but in Virgil's case, good business sense supersedes any tendency toward wanton mischief. I once overheard Virgil talking with a customer who was on his way to fish a nearby lake. The customer—a man who Aldo Leopold would no doubt have described as a gadgeteer—asked question after question, and although Virgil could answer many of them, gradually the questions degenerated into unanswerable generalities. This went on until finally Virgil, in a deadpan voice that did not even hint at jest, asked the customer if he wanted him to go out and fish the lake for him.

After coffee and a breakfast of oatmeal and scrambled eggs, Kim and I loaded up the truck and headed south from Hawley Lake toward Christmas Tree. Rain had fallen for most of the night and now the road was alive and threaded with its water. Due to their ponderous size, ponderosa pines form an open and spacious forest that invites passersby to gaze into its reaches. If I had been in these mountains a few years ago, I might have barreled ahead until I reached my destination. But on this day, knowing we could see a range of animals including turkey, deer, bear, elk, and horses, I drove slowly and quietly. A few minutes later we rounded a curve and caught an elk cow and her calf in the road. The calf was probably born a couple of months ago, a likelihood suggested by its downy fur, size, and lack of coordination, like a deer on stilts. My excitement was tempered, however: One look at the mother and I knew she was stressed. She hesitated as her calf struggled to reach the forest, but after a moment, she bounded into the shadows. I pulled over and gave the calf a chance to get out of the road. When we finally drove out of there, I glimpsed the mother walking deep in the forest, an embodiment of silence and grace.

Kim and I fished Christmas Tree for two days, and during that time we caught around sixty trout, mostly apaches, and we lost or missed half as many. The hatch was on, and if I didn't know better, I'd say that the world's supply of damsels, great blue undulating waves of them, originated here. At these times the apache would feed voraciously, taking drys the instant they hit the water. But they are very efficient feeders, which is likely afforded by such an abundant, albeit ephemeral, food source. Unlike browns, which often leave the water and dive down on topwater prey, the slender and elegant apaches sip the damsels so lightly they may as well be sipping tea.

But then, just as suddenly as the hatch would start, it would stop. During these lulls I would lean back in my tube and enjoy being in a place where everything—including me, most of the time—is at its finest. I recall a conversation I had with a friend a few years ago: After telling her I was a catch-and-release fly fisher, her brow furrowed and she asked how I could fish at all if I cared so much about trout. Catch-and-release or not, she argued, I was still harassing them. I couldn't answer her at the time, but it was an important question then, and it is an important question now.

Today I would evoke Horace and say simply that nature is red in tooth and claw: I fish because it is my nature to do so. But that is only part of the answer. Fly fishing helps me remember I am a citizen and steward of the living world. I fish for trout because I value them, and I value the places where trout live because I fish. As an activity that is inextricably tied to natural places and to their preservation (and to those corresponding aspects of ourselves), fly fishing involves the deep, complex story of the world. Past, present, and future emerge through the experience, like damsels and trout and voices. If I listen closely when I am on the water, I can still hear the wind in far away tree tops. I can still hear the roaring.

The History
of Ice

Nole's house was dark except for the kitchen. I must have seen that exact scene a hundred times, but I never tired of the repetition. I knew that Nole would soon appear on the doorstep holding a duffel bag full of fishing gear in one hand, and a mug of coffee in the other, his white-blond hair going every which way like an Escher drawing. Then he would smile, tip his head, and we'd be on our way. Fly fishing is intensely personal, but I enjoy sharing the experience with people whom I love and trust, and who value the natural world as much as I do. I can count them on one hand. As my teacher and dearest childhood friend, I think of Nole as the thumb on that hand.

I have met some kind and thoughtful anglers on the river. A few have even given me flies or a tug of whiskey from their flask. But for the most part, my sense is that they would rather not see me. I can detect the disposition of another angler from a hundred yards away. Body language—the angle of the head, for instance, or the frequency at which one angler looks at another—is a fairly reliable indicator of an angler's mood. These dynamics are not unlike those encountered by Alaskan brown bears during the salmon run. During this period, these essentially solitary animals gather to feed on the spawning fish, which they accomplish by following relatively predictable yet complex social protocols. When these protocols aren't acknowledged, hackles start rising.

I don't think anglers are fundamentally much different than bears, and the differences that do exist probably have more to do with context, and the form of response to encroachment on that context. The majority of anglers no longer depend on fish as a food source, but bears do: For them the acquisition of salmon is a matter of survival, which is evinced by the fierceness of their territorial displays. Anglers have their displays as well, of course, and they will sometimes inflict psychological wounds, but generally they are like other animals insofar as they try to avoid physical conflict. This explains why anglers like me tend to fish with one or two particular people, if not alone, and why we are seldom happy to see other anglers coming around the bend. Still, I'm not complaining: I've been fly fishing for a decade, and I've only encountered a couple of cranky codgers and a few brazen youngsters. Beyond that, my fishing days have been pleasant and peaceful.

Nole and I were well up Parley's Canyon when the snow stopped falling. We still had an hour of travel ahead of us, which meant we would be on the river at sunrise. By the time we reach the town of Duchesne,

Utah, I will have gained over six thousand feet of elevation above my new home in the Sonora Desert of Arizona. The increase in elevation, coupled with the darkness and the hot air from the heater, lulled me into a state of reflection. I wonder if darkness is not the origin of our first stories. Perhaps our ancestors learned to cope with the dark by attempting to articulate whatever they feared might leap out of it.

Nole is a notorious storyteller, and I had to smile when I recalled a confrontation he had on the Middle Provo River. He was fishing his way off the river when he came to a couple of old fishermen who, in their pressed shirts and unsullied waders, looked like they just leapt from the pages of an Orvis catalog. Local anglers know the run they were fishing as the car hole because the front end of an old Ford protrudes from its bank. This hole is not only the last one before the takeout, it is also a classic, so these old men had planted themselves right in the middle of it.

Seeing they were river walkers—a disparaging label reserved for anglers who destroy riverine habitat by walking through it—Nole (the brazen youth) figured he had license to "flex," which he did by casting to the headwater just above them. But his attempt to oust this pair of old bears was unsuccessful: With an insistent tone, one of the old men wondered if Nole couldn't give them some space and go somewhere else "for Pete's sake." Nole said he retaliated by telling them they weren't going to catch anything anyhow because they were standing in the middle of the goddamn hole. Now both men were looking at him, and the man who had been silent put his hand on his hip. Nole didn't say how he interpreted that gesture, but right after it he reeled in and walked into the willows. Not exactly the fabled camaraderie between anglers, but there wasn't bloodshed either.

Two refills of coffee and a half-hour later, we rounded Strawberry Reservoir. A heavy fog had settled on the road, and as we drove into its heart, I felt like I was flying through a cloud in an airplane. Then the road curved east above the reservoir and the fog cleared. When I saw the water for the first time, I marveled at all that is unknown-and-yet-knowable about the world, and at how much ideas can either nurture or prevent that knowing.

Every country drive has its silent times, those moments in the morning and in the evening when everything glows, the dog is asleep in the back seat, and we dream with our eyes wide open. Though I could not see it, I knew the Strawberry River was running parallel to and south of us as we wound our way toward its source, a place called Starvation Lake. I don't know how the lake got its name, but on that fall day the name seemed particularly poignant. *This is where the wind lives*, I thought, as I looked across the cold, white-lipped water of the lake. Once we crossed a small bridge, Nole pulled to the roadside. The sky was a hard blue, and each time the wind died I felt the sun. I closed my eyes and inhaled deeply: The dry smell of sage and sandstone, and of ice fringing the shore, evoked a menagerie of emotions. But mostly I felt the need to keep moving, until I had reached that place where I could outlast those long dark days of the coming snows.

Duchesne was still except for the exhaust of an old truck idling outside the local gas station. A moment later we were traveling north out of town on an old two-track road that carves through hay fields and fields of sage brush. The road was vaguely silver with frost, so I studied it for wheel tracks, hoping that we had the river to ourselves. As we descended toward the river, we saw a group of groggy longhorns strung along the road. Once we were out of car I scanned the group for calves. After seeing several, I told Nole that he could go through them, but that I was going to cut up the hill and come out ahead of them. *Besides*, I said, pointing to a huge one-ton male standing in the middle road, *take a look at that bruiser*. Nole chuckled, but he didn't protest. As we cut up the hill, the group stopped and watched us, their huge black noses slightly raised to confirm what their eyes were telling them.

We walked briskly up the road toward the dam, out of which flowed the Strawberry River. The sun had risen above the ridge and was heralded

by the lows of cows and the ruckus of courting mallards. I tried to imagine
what this place looked like before the dam was built, and in a few seconds
I had removed the dam and traced the river east along a swath of ancient
cottonwoods until it had climbed into the Uinta Mountains. There it
fanned into cold, clear streams, dozens of them leading back to silent fields
of ice and snow. A large raven croaked overhead. He was at least thirty
feet up and still I could see him looking down at us. I was pleased by the
acknowledgment. Even though some animals may not seem to be aware
of us, in reality they are more aware of us than we are of them. This may
explain why I feel such profound comfort, and why I never feel alone, in
the presence of other animals. Raven or human, we all spend our lives trying to secure ourselves in the world.

Strawberry River isn't much wider than a country road, and its brown
stones are smooth and silt free, but the water was swift and cold. If one of
us were to fall in, the day would be over, so Nole and I held elbows and
cut across the river. Once there, we sat on the bank of the first hole and
watched the water. After a few moments, however, watching became gazing, and had a trout not risen, we might have sat there all day, spellbound.
That would have been fine, too, of course, but there was fishing to do, so I
rolled out line until my nymphs were on a collision course with the feeding
trout. As my indicator passed over the place where the trout had appeared,
Nole encouraged me to get ready.

When nothing happened, he suggested I roll my bugs to the top of the
hole and mend the seam. I did so and midway into the run I hooked up
with a thick, two-pound brown. I have caught browns in many places, but
the browns of Strawberry River are the strongest and the hardest fighting I
have encountered. When I finally brought him in, my arm was exhausted,
but I was joyful. I slipped the fly from his mouth and a minute later, he
swam slowly away from my open hand and down to the river bottom
where he held, barely perceptible, above a bar of green-gold sand, his gill

plates winking in the dark water. Nole was sitting on the bank, and he looked up from studying his flies, smiled, and welcomed me home.

I worked that run for a half-hour, not because it continued to yield fish, but because it faced the sun. I tipped my hat back and basked for a few moments after each cast. A small group of cedar waxwings fed on dry berries in the trees across the river. Nole had worked his way down to the next hole. I could see he had one on, and judging by the bend in his rod, the fish was at least three pounds. Under most circumstances, watching a stranger bring in a fish is about as interesting as watching a stranger win the lottery, but I do enjoy observing my fishing partner come to terms with the creature on the end of his line.

If Nole and I were fishing this river together a hundred thousand years ago, it is likely we would have been members of the same kinship band, in which case each of us would have been interested in the other's capture of prey: After all, if one of us eats, chances are we all get to eat. This scenario would change, however, in the case of a stranger or a member of an unknown band. Territorial complications aside, assuming Nole and I were fishing near this hypothetical stranger, my guess is that the only reason either of us would have been interested in his catch is if we were thinking of taking it from him. Obviously we have come a long way since then: Now we muster as much excitement as we can when someone we don't know catches a fish, or we glance over begrudgingly and think *lucky bastard.*

By the time I had made my way to where Nole was standing, the trout had drifted down river and was holding just above a deep swirl of fast water, on either side of which sandbars had formed and sprouted tangles of roots now drowned by the high water. I pointed out the obvious and warned Nole that he would be in trouble if that trout turned tail and ran that channel. "Don't you worry . . ." but just as he said that his reel popped off and shot out into the river. This could only mean one thing: He had forgotten to tighten his reel seat. "Rookie!" I laughed. To make matters worse, the trout now had some slack, and so he floated back between the two snags. "This is going to be interesting," I said. If someone else were in Nole's position, I likely would have thought *there's no way he's going to bring in that fish,* but in Nole's case I refrained from drawing hasty conclusions.

Insofar as Nole's as graceful as the trout he's got on, watching him angle is like watching Bob Ross paint, except Nole doesn't say "God Bless" each time he releases a fish. But the rest is there: the art and the calm, and the pleasure we feel whenever we witness the workings, fluidity, and mastery of craft. Seeing that the trout was again on the move, Nole took in the slack as he walked into the river. The reel had fallen into about two feet of water, so he had to hold his rod high, pinch off his line, bend down, and pick up the reel while keeping the trout from breaking off or hanging up on a snag. After a couple of minutes, Nole had put on his reel and coaxed the fish to the top of the hole. Then, like a film clip in reverse, Nole backed out of the river, stood on the bank, and brought the fish to hand. "You're a regular Paul Maclean," I said, smiling under my hat. The trout had wrecked Nole's fly, so he clipped it off with his teeth and then looked at me. "Well," he said, "that must make you a regular Norman."

Around noon the snow started falling again and with it came a freezing wind from out of the north. We hadn't caught anything for the last hour. And then there was the hunger. Nole and I decided to wait out the cold and eat our lunch in a cabin someone had built and abandoned in a grove of old cottonwoods just off the river. We ducked inside and sat against the northern wall. The windows were glassless and so the wind came in, passed over our heads, and died somewhere in the cabin. Nole took out a red bandanna, spread it out on the ground and began looking for stones to keep it there. Not much is left of whoever lived here: shards of plates, iron from an old stove, and the desiccated segment of a small picture frame. Fragments of a life. Remnants that, in some way, signify all our lives and the deep water from which they temporarily rise.

The snow began falling in curtains, and apart from the river-roll and the whisper of sleet in the cottonwoods, the day was quiet. I turned up my collar and held my knees. When I was nineteen and didn't give history or silence a second thought, I took several trips to southern Utah. On one occasion I was in Zion National Park with Nole and Kim. We had spent the first day hiking and loafing around the emerald pools. When we got back to camp at twilight, we built a fire, ate, and then went to bed. Sometime after midnight I awoke. The fire was smoldering and everyone was asleep. I hadn't seen that many stars since I was a kid living in northern Maine, so I watched them for a long time.

I remember lying there, all warm despite the chill June night, and finally closing my eyes, relishing the sweet peppery smoke as it drifted over me and, I imagined, into Nole's and Kim's dreams. Then I noticed a ringing. Initially I thought it was in my head, but as I listened, I realized I was not hearing *a* sound, but several sounds that had merged, layers of them, each representing a particular animal—crickets, bats, mice, owls, and toads—that had come out to feed or breed in the cover of night. Whoever lived in this cabin would probably know what I experienced, and so too would the first people to live out here. They slept on deerskins, kept one ear to the ground and one to the sky so they could hear footsteps and horse hooves and stars falling.

The snow had tapered off and Nole had stepped outside and was watching two flurry-swept horses chop at the last sun-browned stubble of grass. A mist had rolled off the river and was hanging in the trees along the pasture. The brunt of the storm had moved on, but the sky remained gray. Nole and I agreed that this was fishing weather. We could have taken a shortcut to the river, a cattle path through a grove of Russian olive trees, but we decided that risking thorn punctures to our waders and bodies was not worth the minutes we would lose by walking across the pasture. As we neared the middle of the pasture, I glanced at the horses—a male and a female—and saw them watching us. They weren't far, and I could see their breath and the long downy hairs of their winter coats. Then they started walking toward us.

I couldn't help thinking of James Wright's famous poem "A Blessing," in which he and a friend have a pleasant encounter with two ponies grazing in a pasture near the highway. But unlike Wright, I didn't get the feeling that these horses were happy to see us. I suggested that possibility to Nole, but he was unconcerned, and so the two of us stood there and waited for the horses to make contact. Horses are, of course, large and powerful animals, and I remember being distinctly aware of our size difference and of the fact that there was nothing to hide behind.

The horses approached Nole first because he was the closest. He spoke to them in low tones and extended his open hand for the male to smell, but the longer I watched, the more I realized that the male—with his flattened ears and standoffish demeanor—didn't want any part of what Nole was offering. Realizing things weren't going to get any better, I started to back off and encouraged Nole to do the same. Initially Nole resisted the idea that we might be in danger, but his resistance didn't last long: Just as soon as we turned our backs to them, the horses closed the space between us, as if to prevent us from turning around to face them. I could hear them breathing, and it took everything I had to keep from running.

In addition to being afraid, I must admit I was somewhat disappointed at the time, if only because Wright and his friend felt welcomed by the ponies. Wright's poem had clearly made an impression on me. Because of it, I was expecting a pleasant encounter. Perhaps the horses perceived us as trespassers, which is why they did not relent until they had driven us out of their territory. But they wanted nothing to do with us.

The appeal of Wright's poem is that in it nonhuman nature actively welcomes us, but of course that is not always what happens. In fact, the more important awareness—and challenge, ultimately—would involve feeling welcome or at home in the *absence* of any overt welcome, which is a purely humanistic notion. Wright's view is beautiful and useful, but it becomes much more so when one sees beyond its romanticism. Lovely as romanticism is, out here it can get you killed. Out here, bodies freeze hard as stone even though the sun is shining.

Coyote
Grammar

When Kim and I left the house in the cool of the morning dark, we could still see the stars. The streets out of town were mostly empty, and because of that emptiness I fantasized that many people had disappeared in the night, and that the world would now recover. Kim yawned and her eyes moistened. I suggested she get some sleep and that I would awaken her once we had climbed to the White Mountains, where we would camp and fish for autumn browns. Two hours later we descended into the Salt River Canyon. Although I could not see it, the sun was up. The river ran thick and red after two nights of heavy rain in the high country. The lakes would be cooler and life more comfortable, I thought. Under the cover of clouds, insects would feel safer to hatch. All life would be living—and eating—fiercely.

After several switchbacks, the road straightened until just before the bridge, which joins the Tonto National Forest and the Apache Indian Reservations. Kim slept with her head against the window. Her mouth was open just enough, and I could see the sun light through her cheek. As we drove out onto the bridge, I saw a coyote pup that was so tranquil and untouched, I thought he was sleeping. Judging by his size and the pinkness of his toes, I guessed he had been born this last spring. Nourished by a supple layer of fat, his coat was silver-tipped and downy. When the wind blew over him, those first soft hairs parted and I could see the still-bright pores of his new skin.

Hunger is constant, but eating is not, so in this season the trout gorge and fatten themselves before the skin of the lake freezes and food becomes scarce. *Salmo trutta* externalizes changes in light and temperature. As autumn nears, their bodies (and my thoughts) begin to darken. Over the course of spring and summer, the earth turns until the sun glides overhead, brightening the water to a pale green. When everything is done, some of the trout appear very much like boreal clouds. Knowing this, the fish hawks migrate here to breed and hunt in the spring, when the earth slips away from the sun and the skies tend to whiten.

Dark above and light below, the fish hawk relates well to sun and prey. Kim has a background in biology, so I ask her if she thinks the bird's white belly evolved as a hunting adaptation. After all, what is more inconspicuous against the sea of all that sky, a black kite or a white kite? She looks up at the left hemisphere of her brain, and her brow furrows as she quickly explores the question. Then she looks at a fish hawk perched in a dead pine tree. A few moments later she says, without a hint of irony, *Evolution is so sexy.*

Fish hawks fly so high their shadows evaporate before they reach the surface, beneath which the trout are in the process of switching skins. Like thousands of reversed dawns, the browns begin turning purple, a process that must enable them to absorb low light levels. This coloration also conceals the trout as they cruise the shoreline for prey. While I've heard of trout whose stomachs have disclosed as many as six mice, crawfish infest most White Mountain lakes and rivers, and so provide an optimal (and problematic) source of food. Just over there, in a few inches of shaded water, a crawdad as big as my hand lies unperturbed in the soft, dark matter. At that size, he can afford to relax. Knowing this species predates the advent of modern humans by at least sixty-five million years excites real perspective. Those are some strong genes, a truth that is substantiated by the armored vehicle used to convey them.

When an aspen leaf rocks onto the water, a thumb-size shellfish—still new at life and very much on the menu—bolts backward toward shore, kicking up a screen of fine loam with two snaps of its powerful tail. The shore is fringed in places by stiff grass, so when a blade of it moves even a little it catches my attention. A blond hopper inches its way up the blade and then leaps. The wind carries him into the water. He kicks once or twice, then stills. I watch him until the wind stirs and he drowns. A bank of clouds drifts between the sun and me. The wind rises. I look out across the water: A pair of mourning cloaks tumble and flash like leaves that will not fall.

Mysticism is the beautiful word for ignorance. After a light rain the sky cleared and I floated out into the cove. The pines creaked as the wind blew through them toward the lake, but no more than a breeze reached me. I dipped my hand in the clear, cold water and patted the back of my neck. Glistening and soft-bodied, a nascent, violet damsel crawled out of the water and onto my tube to dry. I slid my finger under its thorax and he reluctantly climbed aboard. I turned him in the light to admire him. His wings beat and stilled. I saw another damsel basking in the sun, his sleek abdomen slightly curled. I looked for the damsel on my finger, but it was gone.

Kim was fishing the mouth of the inlet. She was upwind, so when she said *Hello, fish, it's been awhile* I could hear her clearly even though I was forty yards away. There was a nice bend in her rod. *What do you have on?*

Once she had brought in the trout and had released it, she called back to me: *A tan damsel nymph.* I heard some splashing and looked up to see a small bird bathing just off shore. When I glassed it, I saw a dark-eyed junco dunking and preening his snow-blue chest feathers. He paused, looked around, shook out his feathers, and then resumed bathing. I am convinced that there are at least two things a person can do if he desires to learn the meaning of his life: He can sit by the ocean at dark, and go birding at dawn.

When I imagine my life as a trout, I see myself holding at the mouth of the cove. I hunt the first seven feet of water, on the threshold of light, and when life crosses into view, I devour it. Having chosen my *human* hunting place, I quickly tied on a tan damsel nymph and sow bug tandem. The fishhooks, thin as eyelashes, reminded me I was rushing. While I waited for my flies to sink, I watched the young osprey watch me from his perch. He seemed to regard me with mild interest, and then he leaned forward and jettisoned a silky white rope of shit into the trees below him. When animals gaze at one another, it usually means—among other things—*I want to eat you* or *I challenge you*, so most animals do not enjoy being stared at, and birds are no exception. The osprey is a supreme judge of distance, however, and I am far enough way that he accepts my presence. Though I know his acceptance of me is conditional, I still feel like I have a place here in addition to the place I imagine.

After eating oranges, smoked herring, rye bread, and two bottles of cold beer, Kim and I leaned back in the soft, dry grass. She extended her arm and slid her hand beneath my head, cradling it, and I did the same for her. Her skull is very round and small, and I remember that it felt cool in my hand. The wind was blowing in the pine tops, and from time to time we would hear a pinecone fall to the earth. I turned my head to look at Kim and I could smell the dark soil and feel the warm grass on my face.

Her eyes were closed and her eyelids trembled. The wind had blown rogue strands of hair across her lips. *I feel you looking at me*, she said. Then she turned toward me and opened her eyes. The wind had all but died, so we could hear a group of mallards foraging just offshore. I sat up to watch them and instead saw a series of rises out in the cove. Then another trout rose a few feet away. I looked back at Kim to see if she were seeing all this. The sun was on her teeth and they looked like they had just been born.

By the time I got into position, the feeding had ceased as suddenly as it had started. The clouds drifted off and the water became very still. Except for the fitful rattle of a belted kingfisher, the woods were quiet. I could smell the vague-but-sweet algae smell of the water. I freed my flies, paid out line, and then rolled my nymphs out into the water. After I was sure the flies had sunk, I started counting to thirty-three, my age at the time. Counting is an effective way to create time (or to encourage patience), but not without consequence: As a series of repetitions, numbers are as incantatory as any mantra, so when I reached twenty-five and my strike indicator disappeared with a small plop, I had counted myself into a state of self-induced trance, a condition generally known by anglers as sleeping.

The loss of a second often means the loss of the trout, but this fish took my fly with such ardor, he essentially set the hook for me. I raised my rod tip and quickly stripped line. Before I could get him on the rod, though, he swam straight toward me in a rush. I said *Smart fish* as I hurried to get in my line, but I could not haul fast enough. All I could do was strip and give line as he dictated, so when he reached the tube and decided to dive straight down, I had no recourse. The instant he reached the end of his run, I knew what he was going to do, but by then he had swum straight up and, having just created ten feet of slack, threw the hook. I leaned back and smiled. Something very old happens when you hook a fish, but something timeless happens when you lose it.

That night we slept in a stand of pines above the lake. When I awoke the next morning it was still dark and my breath came out as mist. A mist smelling of pine and sedge had drifted up from the water and my hair was wet and cold with it. I pulled on my clothes and boots and was about to start the coffee when from down in the forest came a great and sustained grammar of coyote whines, howls, barks, and yips. Then silence and the empty caves of my ears. I stood there, entranced. What had happened out there, just beyond those nearby trees? Then, from the opposite direction, a single howl rose and fell. I urged Kim to awaken, but it was too late. Afterward, I made coffee and eggs by the light of a small lamp. I put a lid on the eggs while Kim got dressed. I thought about the coyote pup on the bridge and all I could say was *sleep on*.

Green River

A Memoir

The air was crisp and stark, and it gave a strange ethereal clarity to the stars and to the somber bellows of trains as they lumbered through town. Two days ago I was hiking near my home in the Sonora Desert in shorts and a T-shirt. Now I was wearing a cable-knit sweater and heavy wool pants from the army/navy surplus store, staring at the cold and snowy Wasatch Mountains, trying to remember my life here, and why I left. I was on my way to fly fish the Green River in far eastern Utah, near the Wyoming and Colorado borders. Nole and I were to meet my old friends Morley and Trevor at the mouth of Parley's Canyon, and from there the four of us would travel, drift boat in tow, to Morley's cabin, which is just up the road from the town of Dutch John. Over the years I had stayed in contact with Nole, but I had seen Morley and Trevor on only a handful of occasions since high school. We had been good friends then, so I was eager to spend time with them and to learn what kind of people they had become. And I suppose I wanted them to know what kind of person I had become after all this time.

I first saw the Green River in 1981. I was thirteen years old. We had lived in Utah for a couple of months when my mother's boyfriend, Phil—or Big Dog, as we used to call him—suggested we go to the Green and do some camping and fishing. My mother agreed and so we packed up the old yellow van and we left the next morning. Having just moved from the deep woods of northern Maine, I was struck by the landscape of the American West, and I remember my first day in Utah, sitting on the curb in front of our new suburban house in late summer, caught between the pleasure of my body—the sweet smell of sage, the deep light, the low sun surrounded by all that sky—and my longing for home.

When I recall that first trip to the Green, however, few memories surface. The Green flows out of Flaming Gorge Dam, so the water numbed our feet even in August. On the second day of our trip, Phil and my brother and I launched a small inflatable raft just below the dam, and we spent the day floating the seven-and-a-half miles to Little Hole. When he wasn't paddling us through the rapids, Phil fished, and I remember him hooking into a huge rainbow trout that he fought gleefully until it leapt from the river and snapped his line. I can still see it shining and arcing, perfectly suspended there, high above the water. Phil just laughed. He was good that way.

Later we went ashore for lunch, and after we had eaten and rested, I decided to walk the trail that follows the river. I had been hearing the buzz of cicadas throughout the day, but now that I was on land, their song was both deafening and hypnotic. I walked for a while, following Phil and Christian's progress as I went. Most of the time we kept an even pace, even though it meant I had to travel at a pace that was between a walk and a run. Eventually they hit some slow water, but I just kept on going until I couldn't see them anymore.

I rounded a bend in the trail and sat on a boulder that overlooked the river. The boulder neighbored a giant ponderosa pine, and its branches were hung with the golden nymphal skins of cicadas, hundreds of them, moving faintly in the breeze like tiny, silent bells. I leaned against the tree and closed my eyes, enjoying the fragrant shade. When I opened them again I saw an enormous, gray-blue fish hovering in the shadow of the rock. Although when estimating the fish's size I must take into account the magnifying properties of water and childhood, the passing of time, and the changeability of memory, I would say the fish weighed no less than twenty pounds, *a baby whale*, I remember thinking then.

A breeze came down Red Canyon and swept through the branches above me, sending pinecones into the water. The big fish was gone, but in its place was a group of kokanee minnows, flinching this way and that like nervous silver. I looked up river just in time to see Phil pull a fish into the boat. He had a good-ol'-boy laugh and a Dutch Boy haircut, and he did a pretty good job with us kids for being a twenty-six-year-old kid himself. I could see my brother watching from the bow, and he shrank back the moment Phil rapped the trout on the head with his huge fist. The trout swished its tail once or twice and then stilled just before Phil laid him in the hull.

What did you catch? I called out. *A keeper,* Phil said, as he used what in his hands appeared to be a ridiculously small oar to cut across the fast water. Christian just shrugged: He could tell you the names of famous skateboarders and punk rock bands, but asking him to identify a fish was like asking him to point out Mars in the light of day. As they neared shore, I could see that the boat had taken on water, a thin film of it rolling back and forth. In all, Phil had caught three cutthroat trout, and except for the most recent, which still held much of its color, they were pale versions of themselves. I remember wondering where their colors went when they died. But I was sure the answer was in the bottom of that boat because of how those trout and my brother's sunburned feet shined after the bloody water had washed them clean.

The longer I live, the more I want to know what is here. I think that is why, over time, I have tried to learn the names of things. I was taught to think that language is ultimately inadequate for expressing the depth of human experience. If that is true, it is to a negligible extent. The real inadequacy may actually lie in our understanding of language and its origins. Now I see words and names as the starting points of knowledge, which connect me to life and help me to love it.

Like the name of the beautifully colored bird I killed as a boy, I had always wondered what type of fish I had seen hovering there in the shadow of that rock, its mouth opening and closing, saying everything and nothing. Years later I would share the sighting with Nole, who speculated the fish was a mackinaw—or lake trout—from Flaming Gorge that had somehow made it past the dam. *How is that possible?* I asked him. He could think of at least three explanations: The timing of the turbines had been just right; someone had planted him in the river; or a fish hawk had dropped him into the river en route to the nest.

Regardless, there he was, mattering in the far away water of nineteen years ago, a huge fish in small water. Nole reminded me of a similar encounter we had on the Strawberry River. We were fishing a long run that spilled into a deep hole before flattening out again. We had been fishing all morning and I was tired, so I reeled in, sat against a log, drew down my hat, and dozed while Nole tried to get himself some honey.

I was half asleep when, in a loud whisper, Nole said: *There's a huge fish over here!* His posture reminded me of a question mark as he leaned over the water, slowly moving his head from side to side to solve the glare. *What kind?* I asked. *Looks like a brown*, he said. Not that it really mattered: A huge fish is a huge fish. But I had been reading about rogues, a term used by biologists to describe browns that, due to their age, size, and experience, have their own unique behaviors. Rogues are, in effect, super trout, trout bordering on the mythical. That is, until now.

Just that morning I had shared my learning with Nole, so he was well aware of the implications of his find. *Where is it?* I asked, careful not to make any sudden movements. As I looked down through the slightly rumpled water, I could see the sandy bottom of the hole and a dark shelf of rock and soil that sloped gently upward before lightening and leveling off into ankle-deep water. *Right there!* Nole said, pointing. *Above or below the shelf?* In an effort to see what I was seeing, Nole moved his head left and right, squatted, and then stood up again. *What shelf?*

When Nole said the fish was huge, I figured he was looking at a five- or six-pounder, which in the context of this river would be huge. Because that's what I was expecting, instead of seeing a three-foot long, roughly fifteen-pound fish, I saw a shelf. Seeing that fish reminded me of drowning in an inch of water: It's hard to imagine it can happen. *It's a rogue!* I exclaimed. The fish had swum a few inches up river, where the water wasn't as clear, so the process of identifying it was difficult. Notwithstanding my desire to gaze at this improbable inhabitant, in a way I wanted to walk off the river at that moment, before anything could undo my belief in what I had just seen.

And yet my need to know with certainty was stronger. Still, we left the river that day without admitting that what we were seeing was actually a sucker fish, but later that night, as I was getting my gear from the back of Nole's car, we finally dispelled the delusion. *That was a sucker,* I said, not quite asking a question. Not quite making a statement, either. Nole looked at me in the rearview mirror. *The puckering lips were a giveaway,* he replied, in the stolid tone of disenchantment. Although an impressive sight to behold, a fifteen-pound sucker is not unusual, really. A hardy and versatile feeder, they can reach up to forty pounds or so. But in a river like the Strawberry, a fifteen-pound brown is as rare as it is beautiful. And except perhaps for death, nothing is more serious than beauty.

The road through southern Wyoming cuts across some of the bleakest country I have ever seen, and as much as I tried to remember that it was late December, and that there was still an unseen and sleeping world beneath those torn sheets of wind-blown snow, I felt an unfamiliar emptiness. As we drove through the small farming town of Mountain View, I could see darkness building to the east. A quiet little town, Mountain View seems very much like a retrospective of early '80s culture. I shared my views with Nole, Morley, and Trevor, and I punctuated my point by tuning in several radio stations, all of which played music from that decade.

Why anyone would choose to hunker down in the '80s is not, however, entirely mysterious. After all, Evanston is not far away. When I was in high school, Evanston was important for one reason: six-percent beer. Crossing the border into Wyoming meant we were crossing into another world, and I remember how peculiar I felt walking out of a roadside gas station with a bag of fireworks in my mouth and a twelve-pack of Mickey Big Mouth under each arm. Evanston was the anti-Utah. Once a thriving coal mining, ranching, and agricultural area, Evanston now feels like a place of desperation, one passed on the way to somewhere else. This notion is supported by countless billboards, the most revealing of which warns passersby to choose Jesus over pornography. Comparatively speaking, then, the '80s must seem innocuous to folks living in little towns like Mountain View, where Boy George, prank calls, and the occasional shit-bagging by the neighborhood kids are just fine, thank you.

Out here, when the sun goes down the people go down with it. Apart from a couple of cars that idled by us, the streets were empty. In Arizona it is the heat that drives people inside. Up here it is the cold. People wear beards, long johns, and turtlenecks. Like Morley. He is two years younger than me but he looks two years older with his gaunt face and tired eyes. That's the outside, but he seems old inside as well. The Morley I saw last was energetic, aggressive, and boisterous. How had he been replaced by the serious and sedate young man who sat beside me now?

Calloused and split by cold, his hands tell part of the story: *When we aren't holding a fly rod, the wife, children, beer, and cigarettes, we pour concrete for a living, now leave us alone.* Morley works the family business, which has kept him lean and strong. This would be my first time drifting a river for the sake of fly fishing, but I already understood the importance of having a powerful oarsman. Including himself and gear, Morley would be responsible for piloting a twenty-one foot craft loaded with roughly seven hundred pounds of cargo. Then I thought of Phil guiding my brother and me down the river, breathing heavily through his nose as he carved the water with those plastic oars. And I knew why he quieted whenever he saw the river whiten.

The sky was storm-gray and out of it came flakes of clean white snow, large flakes like those caught on the tongues of children. The snow dusted whatever would let it: the high dead blades of roadside grass; the roofs of houses poised like hands in prayer; the back of a dog that slept on a porch. We were still two hours away from Morley's cabin, and he wondered aloud if the roads there would be clear. The cabin and surrounding acreage has been in his family for five generations, and during that time there had been essentially no development. As far as I could tell, the Morleys wanted it that way.

At the end of town is a little one-room liquor store called the Crow's Nest, and as we neared it Morley glanced at his watch and announced it was beer-thirty. The store was still glowing with hundreds of Christmas lights and an electric Santa that stood on the rooftop, beaming with arctic jubilance. Then the drive-up window slid open and the clerk asked for our order. Morley looked up at Santa and said *Give us a case of whatever he's been drinking.*

I awoke the next morning to the smell of coffee and last night's fire. Above my head a small window dripped with dew. Someone was sleeping hard in the bed across from me, and although his head was under the covers,

I realized it was Trevor because his feet overshot the bed by a good six inches. I slipped out of my sleeping bag and dressed in layers of cotton, fleece, and wool. As I left the room I shook Trevor's foot and told him the trout weren't going to catch themselves. He must have already been awake because he snapped the covers from over his head and said that if the trout were to catch themselves, they'd have him to thank for it.

Morley sat tying flies at the kitchen table. Spread out before him was an alchemy of fishhooks and beer bottles, spools of thread, cards, coffee cups, feathers, and cigarettes. *How'd you sleep,* he asked, keeping his eyes on his work. I poured myself a cup of coffee. *Deeply,* I said. *No dreams? Not that I remember.* He nodded and raised his brow as he trimmed his fly. *Is that surprising to you? A little,* he said. *Usually newcomers dream pretty hard up here.* I sat at the table and watched Morley tie a leech pattern known as wooly bugger. Nole had slept on the couch near the woodstove, and I could see him repositioning himself so as to shun the conversation and sunlight that now filled the room.

Rise, old man Walkingshaw, I said. Nole sat up and kicked off his covers. *I dreamt of something warm and friendly,* he said with a sheepish grin. His cheek and forehead wore the imprint of his sleeping bag's zipper, and his long blond hair appeared to have been electrocuted. He looked like the bride of Frankenstein's monster. We had only so much daylight, so Morley urged us to prepare our gear and load up the boat. I asked him if he could navigate the river in the dark. He smiled and said that he could, but that in this case it's better to have sex with the lights on.

The night before, Morley had called the lodge at Dutch John and had arranged for a shuttle driver to meet us at the launch ramp at 8:00 a.m. *You think he'll be on time?* I asked. *No question about it,* Morley said. *It's easy money.* For forty dollars he would shuttle the truck and trailer down to the take-out at Little Hole. True to Morley's prediction, the driver was there when we arrived, as were two other men who had just launched their boat. Morley signaled to the driver and then swung around the boat and backed it into the water as Nole, Trevor, and I watched. The temperature was just above freezing and the sky was hazy, and though the sun was out I could not feel it.

Once the boat was tied off, Morley organized the gear so that the weight was evenly distributed. Then he called for us. We climbed in, took our seats, and the driver set us adrift. Directly behind us the dam rose five hundred feet. As much as I tried not to, I imagined all that water—over three million cubic feet of it—pressing against the forty-year-old structure. The deep green water boiled at the base of the dam and then swirled into an eddy that circled and rode high on the cliff wall. Morley decided to give the boat ahead of us plenty of space, so he buried the oars and rowed us into the eddy's eye where the water was clear and calm.

You can't catch a fish if your line's not in the water, he said, as he cupped his lighter and lit a cigarette. Trevor sat behind Morley in the stern, where there was too little room to cast. *I'll sit this one out,* he said, his neatly trimmed, whiskey-colored beard evoking the pelt of a small mammal. Morley handed him a beer and the two sat watching as Nole and I stripped out line and rolled our bugs into the hole. My bugs hadn't been wet for three minutes when I got a strike.

I set the hook and after a brief struggle brought a beautiful rainbow to hand. I leaned over the starboard side, pinched the hook between my fingers and slid it from the trout's mouth. The trout seemed dazed until the moment I removed the hook, at which point it flipped its tail and splashed me before disappearing. Nole leaned over the side and smiled at me. *That's trout for fuck you very much.* Trevor and Morley laughed, and as a gesture of thanks they each poured a swig of beer into the river. In hindsight, I probably should have done the same. The Green boasts anywhere from 3,000 to 9,000 trout per mile, but that was the only trout I caught the whole day.

I am not superstitious . . . unless I am fishing, and then, sometimes without even realizing it, I indulge in any number of fictions. A few years ago my mother gave me a tie tack of a golden trout that belonged to my grandfather. I didn't know my grandfather very well, but I remember him taking me fishing once or twice on the Snake River when I was five or six years old, and that a few days before he died he asked my mother if she thought there were any fishing holes in heaven. Because he was a fisherman, I've always liked to believe I would be safe as long as I was wearing his tie tack in my hat. My mother told me he was deeply afraid of dying, and he loved to fish, so it makes sense to me that he'd want to haunt this old earth, and hang around the fishing holes, even if he does so only in my mind.

Although I am comforted by the idea that my grandfather is watching out for me, I would never count on it. Out here, the mind tells stories. Sometimes the stories help us to stay alive. More often than not, however, we take our stories *to* the river rather than *from* it, and they usually tell us more about the person that's generating them than they do about the actual world. My story about my grandfather is a case in point. But whatever happens on the river is of the river, and that is all that really matters. Today the water is right around forty-five degrees and the air is freezing, and no thinking person would be out here with the delusion that he was special.

The river had rolled wide and smooth for the last two miles, so even from a distance of several hundred yards I could see the water swell and whiten as it flowed over the hidden boulders of Mother-in-Law Rapid. Morley had been leaning on the oars, rowing only when we drifted off the run we were fishing. Now that we were nearing the rapids, he chugged his beer and threw the can in the bow. Nole and I were sitting slightly off-kilter, and as Morley dropped the oars into the water and began to position us for the line he had chosen, he told us to reel in and sit centered. The river had cut a narrow channel, and on one side of it the water quickly became shallow, exposing rocks that most of the year are covered by high water. The other side pounded against the canyon wall and couldn't have been more than three feet wide, much too narrow to permit safe passage of our boat.

Except for that first trip down the Green almost twenty years ago, I had no experience with white water. I grabbed the gunwales and surveyed each shore in the event I were to go overboard. I could see an enormous boulder right in the middle of the channel. *What the hell is that?* I asked, pointing to a battered piece of metal wrapped around the boulder. *That's somebody's boat,* Morley said. We were not five feet from the rapids when Morley dug in the oars and rowed us *up* river. *The boat's not right,* he yelled. A moment later he lifted the oars and we shot down the rapid. The bow dipped and rose and then sliced into a long hump of water, sending up fine white spray. Trevor called to me and hollered as if he were riding herd. I glanced back at him and Morley. They were still the boys I knew.

The sun had passed over us and was now poised on the rim of the canyon's west wall. Morley put us ashore on the eastern side so that we could enjoy a late lunch in what was left of the day's warmth. We would have to make good time from here on out, he said. We had only traveled about five miles in as many hours, and I don't think any of us could have predicted how cold it would be. And it was going to get colder. Snow had fallen the night before, and where the snow ended and the shallows began, a film of ice creaked as the water ebbed beneath it. We each sat on a rock facing the sun, watching to see what the other had brought to eat. The week before, a friend of Nole's had gone salmon fishing in Alaska, and he had been kind enough to share his catch. Nole handed me the sack of fish, and I took a chunk and passed it on. The salmon was smoked to an ember-orange, and the flesh was moist and delicious. I thanked him for the beautiful food and asked for more. Nole flashed his teeth and they were full of salmon. Then he pointed across the river. *Look*, he said.

A golden eagle was perched on a boulder, eating a cottontail rabbit. He held the rabbit with one talon as he tore off a strip of glistening meat, tipped back his head, and chugged it down. I looked at the chunk of salmon in my hand and I wondered what it would mean to know the whole animal again; to hunt and to kill; to open the belly and to feed, broken, ecstatic, face aglow with blood. I would have learned to revere that animal whose own struggles would have so closely mirrored my own.

By the end of the day, Morley had guided us down seven miles of river and ten rapids. And he hadn't even wetted his line. The last quarter mile or so was smooth water with few hazards, so Morley agreed when Nole offered to take over. I was glad he did, because not only did Nole say he had some experience, but Trevor was on his sixth Wyoming beer, and I was so cold I couldn't feel my feet anymore. The sun was long gone and the sky had turned overcast, and all I wanted was to get out of that boat and take off my boots. We drifted passed Catwalk Shoal and rounded the last corner before the take-out at Little Hole. Whoever named the Green River did not name it after the sun had gone down. From dusk on, the river is so black that only someone who knows it well can tell if it's two inches or twenty feet deep. There's something unfathomable about the surface of a river at night. Something best contemplated from shore.

Morley stood in front of me, pounding the banks with a streamer. Shore was a good fifteen yards away, and I could hear his line whip past my head as he hauled it in and threw it out. *Mend that line*, he said to Trevor, whose line stretched and bowed some thirty feet across the water. As Trevor reeled in, he realized he had a fish. The trout came without a fight, which suggested it had been on the line for some time and was now exhausted. Nole was sitting between Trevor and me so I told Trevor I'd release the fish. After I had slipped the hook from the trout's mouth, I held him along side the boat, hoping he would revive. A few seconds later, the trout suddenly surged with energy and broke free of my hand. I watched him glide just below the surface. But then he started to sink into the darkness, and just before he sank from sight he turned belly up, igniting the water.

Sorry darlin', I whispered. I washed my hands in the river and slid slowly back to the center of the boat. *Did you get him off all right?* Trevor asked. Before I could answer, Morley used his rod to point to a twenty-foot wide shoal that divided the river. He warned Nole to stay outside of it because the inside line was coming up too fast, and there would not be time to position the boat. Nole dropped the oars and pushed, but they had not gone deep enough, and they skipped across the water, causing him to fall forward. He recovered quickly and dug the oars in hard, but the boat did not respond. The river was moving faster now and the current was too strong. A moment later we struck the rocks, at which point we all fell silent.

Driving back to the cabin that night, I tried to understand what had happened out there on the water. After all, the boat was fine apart from a few scratches, and at that point we weren't really in any danger. Still, I could not look anyone in the eye. The trouble came when I thought about what might have happened had the circumstances been different. The river itself is dangerous, of course, but the cold was by far the greatest threat, and had someone fallen in the water a few miles up river, far away from help, hypothermia would have likely followed, and there would have been little any of us could have done about it.

Because of this reality, I felt gratitude toward Morley for getting us safely down the river. But I also felt embarrassed for Nole, which wasn't easy. He just stared out the window. I could see his face whenever the moon broke through the clouds. Unless they belong to us, we tend to ignore the silences in our lives, of which there are millions, each with its own meaning, its own voice, and, if we do not learn to listen, its own consequences. But for the man who's silent after being tested by the river: Better put an arm around him.

The next day we slept in late, especially Morley, who staggered into the kitchen about an hour later than the rest of us. Late in the mountains usually means around 8:00 a.m., so even after spending the morning lounging by the fire drinking coffee and talking, we still had the entire day ahead of us. We all agreed that fishing was out of the question. Morley was exhausted, and fish or no fish, we had all had our fill of the cold. Instead, we decided to ease into the day, have breakfast, get our things together, and then go for a walk before making the four-hour trip back to Salt Lake. After the strain of yesterday, I appreciated stretching out on the couch in the warmth of the cabin, listening to the fire and to the talk and laughter of young men who, like me, are living their lives the best they know how, and who were taught by parents who did the same, and so on, beyond anyone's ability to remember.

But we taught each other, too, about failure and gain and fear and love. And about what it really meant to be a man at a time when so few options were available. I thought about these things as we walked across the frozen snow toward the cliffs behind Morley's cabin. And I considered asking them what kind of men they thought they had become. But mostly I wondered if I had been good enough to the world and to my friends, and if I had loved them on their own terms. *What can you do about it now?* I asked myself. I stood beneath a ponderosa pine and looked around. Old fox tracks dimpled the snow. Nole, Morley, and Trevor had gone ahead, but once they realized I wasn't with them they stopped and waited for me to catch up. *What can I do now?* I asked again, jogging across the snow.

This, I said.

Just this.

Linear Drift

Reflections on Pacheta Lake

Floating out here on this mountain lake, I am learning to resolve the contradictions of contemporary life, and how to live responsibly in a world I will inhabit for such a short time. It is spring in the Whites. The roads are clear but snow still holds along the southern end of Pacheta Lake. The air is heavy with the smell of snowmelt and childhood.

Each year, millions of people leave the cities and suburbs to visit our national parks and forests, presumably as a reprieve from their daily lives. Given this need for distance from familiar surroundings, I am always puzzled when I see people driving entire homes into the wilderness. The roads into Pacheta do not permit safe passage to recreational vehicles or RVs. And it has little to do with the size of the vehicles: Logging trucks race along these mountain roads as though they were on tracks. But they are crude and designed to withstand rough terrain. RVs have sophisticated yet fragile suspensions so the bumps in the asphalt don't jostle Earl's hemorrhoids (which he got from sitting too much), interfere with satellite reception, or disturb the Lhasa Apso sleeping on the dashboard.

I am not going to rub two sticks to make fire. Instead, I will decide whether what I have is proportionate to what I need. That is one of the things I admire about Paul Maclean in *A River Runs through It*. He wore his flies in his hat, and he could put everything else important—cigarettes and matches—under it. Then he'd pull it down tight. That is all he needed to fish the waters of Montana. No $700 waders or designer polarized glasses, no fish-finder, and no felt-soled boots. No gadgets. Just a rod, line, leader, a few standard flies, and a love of seeking. Of course some of these novelties were not available during the 1930s. Regardless, I am fairly sure Maclean would have felt a mild disdain for the technicians of modern-day fly fishing, and their $1,000 rods and fifty-pocket vests filled with forty pounds of gear.

Insofar as I believe city things ought to be left in the city, I suppose I too am somewhat of a naturalist. I prefer the mountain sounds—whirr of insects, call of birds, trickle of water, rush of wind, pounding rain and thunder. I prefer silence. I crave the nonhuman drama. Several years ago my friend Bart and I traveled to the Black River. On the map, the Black is about an inch to the south of Pacheta Lake, but the country between the two is mountainous and, in many places, impassable except by a network of often unmarked, labyrinthine four-wheel drive roads. Oddly, the roads seem to have had minimal effect on the area, and though there is no argument that the Black would be better off without them, the area is still one of the most remote and beautiful places in the state. The White Mountain and San Carlos Apache Indian Reservations share the river as a border, and together the tribes control thousands of square miles of pristine forest and desert. It is also true that the San Carlos reservation is not even a third of what it was when it was created in the mid-nineteenth century.

Still relatively untouched, however, the river and the surrounding area is prime habitat for several species, including black bear. After fording the river several times, Bart and I decided on a campsite. We had gotten a late start, so it was nearly dark by the time we arrived. Bart had been drinking all day so I gave him the rote task of gathering firewood while I unloaded the truck and set up camp. As we sat by the fire that night, the subject of bears came up and I told Bart what I knew. He was unconcerned, as was I, although for different reasons: Bart was pie-eyed drunk. As of that trip, I hadn't yet encountered a bear. But I knew prevention—a clean camp and a clear head—was the best defense.

Bart could no longer speak in complex sentences, but he managed to suggest we turn on the truck stereo and listen to some music. I briefly considered his request and then said, "I don't think so." I explained to him that I drove five hours to hear the Black and nothing else. I made the point that any music other than the music of the place simply didn't appeal to me. "Besides," I continued, "if a bear comes around I want to know about it, don't you?" Bart's eyes crossed slightly and he blinked as though a very bright light had just blinded him. I felt a little embarrassed by my insistence because I am usually very accommodating. But I have limits.

To help Bart understand my reasoning, and to help him forget what he thought he was missing, I recounted a hike I had taken a few years back with two writer-friends of mine. The three of us had just started graduate school, so that first year we rarely found time to explore the desert. When I wasn't studying or writing, I was working for my landlord. The job was mindless, but I worked with an interesting guy named Chris Hartford, who would take me to local swimming holes and other secret places in the desert. A stretch of Queen Creek was one of them.

One April morning, when the creek was still flowing with spring run-off, I invited my two fellow graduate students, Rigo and Patty, on a hike to a small swimming hole some local kids had made by damming the stream. Skilled engineers, the kids had piled river rocks a few yards down from where the canyon narrowed and dropped, forming a small waterfall that had carved the riverbed into a bowl. Together with its rich flora, insects, and birds, the creek was a sensory feast. I don't think we had been there for five minutes when, in my elation, I looked over at my friends to see their expressions. "What the fuck are you guys doing?" I asked, taken aback. They put down their books and looked at me. "What's the problem?" Patty asked. "You're surrounded by *living* poetry and you're *reading?*"

I felt like I was witnessing some lame throwback to the Romantic poets. The only things missing were the laudanum, champagne, and lobster salad. "Yeah, so what?" Rigo said, holding his hand above his eyes, blinking and squinting. "You've got all this content, and you've got your nose in a book," I said, annoyed and, I admit, a little wounded. As I told the story, Bart's upper body gyrated. Had he been standing, I'm sure he would have fallen into the fire. I wasn't sure if he saw the parallel or not, but I didn't push it. In the end, the Black spoke for itself: A few minutes later, something—probably a deer or javelina, maybe a bear—crashed through the brush just beyond the firelight. Bart bolted toward the truck. For being pie-eyed drunk, he was surprisingly nimble. I just sat there and laughed. Nothing sobers like adrenaline.

After several hours on Pacheta Lake, my thoughts were odd and sluggish. I wasn't so far gone that I couldn't recognize my confusion as the very early stage of hypothermia. I kicked toward shore and spun my outspread arms to get the blood moving. Remoteness is relative, but out here it's important for things to go well. After a few minutes of walking around, I was fine. But during my early days of learning to fly fish, in my enthusiasm I stayed out longer than any sensible person should, my hip boots full of water, my entire body shivering as the sun went down.

At the other extreme is the arguably lesser threat of dehydration. Strangely, the reality of dehydration seems to have lost meaning in the Southwest vernacular, which is a little like frostbite losing meaning in the Antarctic, or of sunburn losing relevance in Death Valley. We live with certain words and ideas as though they had no counterpart in the physical world. At least that is the way it was with me before I had experienced dehydration, not in the relative safety of the city, but deep in the mountains, seventy miles away from help. I was fishing Pacheta a couple summers ago with Kim and her brother James when it happened, so I guess I wasn't entirely without help. I awoke that morning, chugged some coffee, and left camp without eating breakfast. I should have known I was heading for trouble.

I was already dry as a bone from the day and the night before. We had arrived at noon and fished until dark, and for that seven-hour period, I didn't drink much water, even though I was losing a great deal from sweating. I clinched the deal that night, when I threw back a few beers, again without replenishing my fluids. So the next morning it was only a matter of minutes until I started feeling . . . well, wrong. I spent more than a few minutes in a dilapidated outhouse. A robin had made a nest in the corner and a single chick peered down at me. At my feet was a dead chick. Its sibling might have forced it from the nest, or it may have simply fallen. In any event, sick as I was, I felt it was important not to startle the surviving chick, which might cause it to fall out of the nest. Luckily for the bird, I quickly realized I wasn't going to solve my problem in the outhouse, at which point I mustered a weak "Good luck, little fella," pulled up my waders, and walked out.

I know my body fairly well, but I didn't know this feeling. I sat in the shade of a giant ponderosa pine and tried to figure out what was happening. I glanced back at the outhouse and saw the mother robin perched on the open outhouse door, watching me. She would chirp every few seconds, I assumed, to reassure her chick, which had just had the misfortune of my company. James was oblivious, but Kim, who had just gotten out on the water, read my body from twenty-five yards away. She asked me what was the matter. I wanted her help, but I remember struggling to describe my symptoms, as if talking about them would make them worse. My hesitation was enough to communicate distress, apparently, because Kim reeled in and came to shore.

After sharing a few details—the acid taste in my mouth, slight nausea, no saliva—and recounting the events of the day before, we decided I was dehydrated and probably hungry. Naming what ailed me was a great help: Psychologically, I felt like I had gained some control and could now sip water to get physical results. We left our boats and walked around the lake toward camp. I spent the next three hours lying in the back of my truck, sipping water and eating watermelon, trying to restore my fluid levels.

But to quote Robert Lowell, my mind wasn't right. My anxiousness was compounded by the wind, which was blowing very hard, sending up dust and turning the once placid lake into a litany of whitecaps. And with the wind came the threat of a summer storm. I could see the subtle worry in Kim's face and I was unsettled by it. I think James must have finally tuned in to the emotional weight of that afternoon because he just sat and watched, childlike. Every now and then he'd look at the water and comment on the size of the waves.

Eventually I got it together: I reasoned that the physical part of the problem was being treated. Now what I needed was to get my mind in order, which I did by concentrating on my breathing, as well as by working step-by-step through the worst-case scenario, and then by responding to each problem. The process exhausted me, but at the same time it was reassuring. I asked Kim how she was doing. I knew the experience had taken a toll on her, too, so I encouraged her to share her feelings. Turns out she had employed some creative visualization of her own. "I had a plan," she said, looking directly at me, "I would have taken care of it." The wind knocked over the chairs and sent James scrambling into his tent for cover. I smiled at Kim, closed my eyes, and then drifted into sleep.

Since that experience, I pay close attention to my body, and I am much more careful: I need to be alive come October, when the leaves redden and my son breathes air for the first time. I called Kim on the walkie-talkie and asked her how she was doing. At five months pregnant, comfort is still possible. She's lying on her side, reading and dozing. *Baby loves this mountain air*, she says, sleepily. *Makes him hungry.* The sun had sunk below the tree line. *Copy that*, I said, *I'm on my way.* When I got to shore and stood up, even with four layers of clothes to protect them, my legs felt stupid with cold. I leaned my float tube against a pine and watched the violet green swallows careen and flit above the water, their milky bellies catching the pale blue twilight. I marveled at the precision of their flight, at their ability to fly so fast and close without colliding.

Swallows fly en masse because their prey—mayflies, midges, and the like—appear in droves. Like other animals, mayflies hatch toward dusk and in numbers so as to minimize the threat of predation. In addition to being nimble flyers (how else could they catch such fleeting meals?), swallows must have developed fine-tuned senses. My eyes must be a thousand times bigger than theirs and I can't see the insects they are eating. I've seen swallows swoop past my fly, examine it, and, once they determined it was forgery, fly away. They are remarkably discriminative.

James said he couldn't see his fly anymore. He called to me from down shore, where he probed the banks with a dry fly, hoping for a cruising brown trout. He was far enough away I couldn't see his mouth moving. I waved him in for dinner. Then I closed my eyes and listened to the swallows: Sight is not their only navigational instrument. Perhaps they avoid collision because their wing-beats and twitter are a kind of touching, a physical music that guides and protects their flight.

Back at camp, the three of us prepared soup and sandwiches, a meal whose preparation would still leave us time to take a walk before dark. Down in the valley, I rarely feel true hunger. Food is so available that my stomach is seldom empty. Then there is the slow, if not indeterminate expenditure of energy derived from that food. In the mountains hunger is *the* force. The drive to mate may rival the intensity of this need, but not its duration. The cycle of hunger, feeding, and energy is seamless. Nothing is wasted.

Excluding wartime, America does not kill well. In our local grocery stores, the butchers butcher behind closed doors. For our convenience, they estrange the animal from its original form. The processes remain abstract. If we put our minds to it, I am afraid we could convince our children that the butcher's apron is white and that vast herds of Big Macs roam just beyond the city lights, there for the taking. Most of us do not revere the pig when we eat the ham sandwich. And the blessing is no consolation.

In the mountains, I begin to understand the confusion between consumption and fulfillment. When I think of all the early photographs I've seen, I cannot recall a single fat settler or American Indian. Those men and women were lean with the engagement of the land. They were chiseled and fierce because that is how the land made them. Now work makes most of us soft and full of longing; it gives us bad eyes and hearts, swollen ankles, and double chins. The settlers' lives may have been hard, but I'm sure our own lives are too easy in many respects, and we are the worse for it.

Chilled from being out on the water, James and I peeled off our waders and ate our soup at the fire. James is as odd as they come. At twenty-five, tattoos cover his arms and legs. His favorite is of a topless girl who looks like she belongs on one of those hotrod calendars I have seen hanging on my mechanic's wall. Her jeans have self-made tears on the thighs, apparently in accordance with early '80s Rocker fashion. A red ball cap turned to one side rides high on her head of long, strawberry blond hair. In short, she's a big-boobed, blue-eyed bimbo. A regular country girl with her thumbs in her pockets.

Then there's his tattoo of a toddler wielding a double-barrel shotgun. The bubble above his head says "Let's play." In the words of my father-in-law, James is a real hummer. He's sweet and lazy as smoke, and yet I don't think he has an ounce of fat on him, and not because of his work:

As a truck driver he lives a fairly sedentary lifestyle. My father-in-law, who because of a stroke has a gut like bag of water and walks like a duck with a bum leg, likes to warn James of the day when—five or six years down the road—his "asshole will slam shut" and he'll start packing on the pounds. At those times I pat James on the shoulder and tell him to enjoy his wholesome diet of steak and Pepsi while it lasts.

I remember seeing a PBS special called Frontier House a few years ago. The program followed the day-to-day lives of two families who agreed to live as settlers did during the nineteenth century. One family consisted of a couple, their daughter, and her friend. A few months into the show, the narrator said that the man, who was shown standing in a field wearing only boots and trousers held up by suspenders, was convinced he was starving to death. He looked a little crazed, but a doctor's examination revealed no nutritional deficiencies.

In fact, the doctor concluded that the man was in much better condition than when the show began. Later, during the show's conclusion, we visited the man and his family after they had returned to their normal lives. The man looked like a balloon wearing a three-piece suit. He sipped a glass of red wine as he gazed out enormous windows. The sea was in the distance. Then he smiled wryly at the camera and lifted his glass, his rubicund cheeks inflating into shiny nubs of flesh.

In the wilderness, I see what it means to work for a living. That afternoon I watched a red-faced warbler flit along shore in search of food. Were it not for his namesake, the warbler would be a blur in the failing light, a trick of shadow and light. Alert and attentive, he appeared to stand watch as his mate bathed and preened. Every so often, a western tanager would appear, its uncanny display of orange and yellow and black contrasting sharply with the emerald green leaves, which the tanager combed for delicate, soft-bodied insects. Red-skimmer dragonflies darted by like reflections of red light, snatching and feasting on nearly imperceptible flies. Below I saw a brown trout finning through the shallows, seeking fry to cannibalize. The water whirled and boiled as the trout drove the fry shore-ward. The group split left and right, but one fry jumped out of the water and landed on shore, where it flopped and sucked the new and useless air.

After devouring our soup, James and I scrambled down Pacheta stream, which flows for about a month each spring. Full dark was an hour away but the sky was already sliced with a waxing moon. When I paused to search a deep pool for trout I could hear the somber calls of coyotes. How is it possible that the sounds of animals so different from us can evoke such strong emotions? This time of year night falls slowly in the mountains. Dusk settles in the eyes like a haze of blue smoke. The edges of trees, rocks, plants, and water begin to soften and merge. The songs of day birds yield to the songs of night and the frogs and crickets sing sex and warning in the damp grass. I tell James that we ought to turn back soon: "Not much moonlight tonight," I said, leaping from stone to stone. I could feel the soup sloshing in my stomach. James looked at me blankly. "We'll just follow the stream," I reassured him. I came to a scree field of moss-covered granite. A fallen ponderosa pine lay at its edge, beyond which the stream corridor widened into a meadow of lush grass. James was a few yards behind me, and as I waited for him I glanced at what I thought was the sand-colored hind end of an elk.

I had been seeing elk sign, but in the failing light I didn't think to check it for freshness. I turned to James and put my finger to my lips, then pointed through the trees. "Elk," I said, silently. James's eyes widened and he crouched down as he neared me. "I don't see anything," he whispered. "There," I said, pointing, "behind that tree." We were only twenty yards away, but the dead pine hid us from the elk's already poor vision and, more importantly, we were down wind. After a moment I realized the elk was a young bull, maybe six hundred pounds. His antlers were in the velvet, and I could hear him tearing away at the thick grass. "There's another one," James said, excitedly. "And another," I replied. In all, we counted eight bull elk, each of which would suddenly appear, even though they had been there the whole time. We had been watching them browse for few minutes when James stepped on a dry branch. The males farthest away from us kept on feeding: Apparently they hadn't heard the branch snap. But the male I had seen first lifted his massive head and turned in our direction.

I could see his huge ears working the sound waves for danger. I knew he couldn't see us from that distance if we remained still, but then he must have caught wind of us because he grunted and alerted the others. They stood there for a moment, listening, watching for any movement. Then they bolted into the trees. Elk are enormous and powerful animals, and when they ran I could hear every pound of them bearing down on the mountain. I could *feel* them running. Not their vibrations as they traveled through the ground—I was too far away for that—but the motion and rhythm of their bodies, which I registered in my shoulders, torso, and groin.

Perhaps my impulse was to give chase, or to flee, or to run for the pleasure of running. I'm not sure. In fact, I didn't even realize I had had this reaction until later that night, after I had climbed out of the truck and stood naked beneath the stars, pissing and thinking about those elk. It was as though their movements, and the sound of their hooves crashing into the earth, had for those few moments awakened a relation long dormant in me.

The next morning I woke late and fished for only three or four hours before calling it quits. I could see thunderheads forming in the east. I figured we had an hour or so until the storm reached us. I didn't want to break camp in the rain, so I headed toward shore while James and Kim fished their way back from the other side of the lake. James is fearless, sometimes to a fault, so for his and Kim's safety, I called Kim on the walkie-talkie and reminded her to keep an eye on the sky.

I took one last look at the sky and got busy. Now and then the wind picked up and I could smell the rain coming. By the time Kim and James got to shore, I had everything loaded except for their gear. The rain blew in just as we were leaving, sheets of it, drops so large Kim refers to them as "dollops." Ten minutes down the road we came to a crossroads where we could go north toward White River, or loop east toward Reservation Lake and Show Low. We might have considered taking the northern route, but no one said so. The road is direct and more appealing scenically, but it is twenty-five miles of rough and dangerous terrain. A tire and nerve shredder.

The storm had moved off to the south, and as we drove east toward Reservation Lake and, farther on, civilization, I recalled the last time Kim and I took the northern route home. The last six or seven miles are particularly narrow, steep, and wooded. We were both excited because we had just seen a group of three enormous bull elk a few miles back. Then we came to a hairpin curve, and as we rounded it a black mare and her foal were about to enter the road.

The mare was in front and alongside the foal, and in one fluid motion she turned him out of the road and into the woods. I probably wasn't going twenty miles an hour, but the timing was such that I couldn't even brake, and if she hadn't turned him at that moment, I would have hit them. As we rolled by, I looked into the trees. I expected to see the horses standing there, waiting for us to pass. But they were on the move. *Take me with you,* I remember thinking as the horses faded into the trees.

Run.

Part III
THE AFTERGLOW

Yah, mon. Been goin home all of my life, seem like,
and dis time I meanin to remain.

—PETER MATTHIESSEN

Swan Song

The wetlands lay black and still except for where the cattails pitched along the river like unlit torches. Raucous calls of yellow-headed blackbirds merged with the river-roll in the sedge grass and, high above, the honks of geese that drifted like a scrawl of smoke out of the southern gloaming. As we pulled up to the river, I could see a hazy map of stars in the west, the celestial plot points by which roughly 250 species of birds find their way back to the Bear River Migratory Bird Refuge each year. How many generations of anglers have likewise journeyed to the Bear to ply their lines and reap the silver gifts of water?

I hadn't seen Derek in years, but he looked the same once there was enough light to see him by: thin brown hair, broad shoulders, weathered hands, soft spoken. While I pulled on layers of clothes, he walked to the river and stood there talking . . . to Nole? Himself? The fish? In the cold April morning I watched his breath and fancied I was seeing the commingling souls of words that were hidden to all except me. *What beautiful nonsense*, I said to myself.

Derek blew into his cupped hands and asked Nole what he thought we should do. The two appeared uniform in their chest waders, fleece, and wool. But further study revealed subtle distinctions: Wearing a red bandanna around his neck and a floppy, old hat, Derek could rightly claim the urban cowboy look. On the other continent, Nole could have been on safari in his khaki chest waders, olive-green sweater, and beige vest. And what would the great hunter be without an 8-weight rod in his hand, or what Nole calls his big gun of freshwater fly fishing?

Wipers are a hybrid species, a Frankenfish, as it were, an ichthyologic concoction: A cross between a male white bass and a female striped bass, wipers can reach up to twelve pounds and are very aggressive. Wipers also exhibit sophisticated social behaviors, such as hunting together and thereby capitalizing on the strength of numbers, a notion supported by their tendency to collectively herd shad to the surface. Having no place else to go, the shad are devoured in a frenzy.

Of course, before fishing the Bear the only wipers I had heard of were the kind on my windshield. "Will I need one when I'm older?" I facetiously asked Nole the night he invited me to join him and Derek on the Bear. "Or is it that wipers effectively *wipe* other fish from the face of the Earth?" Although I probably deserved otherwise, when it was time to fish Nole didn't give me any trouble. "Wrong tool," he said, just as I had slipped my 6-weight from its case. "I can't fish this?" I asked. "Nope," he said. "Let me show you why."

Nole leaned into the van and dragged out a big black duffle bag. He unzipped it and took out a tackle box of the variety I had not seen since I was a kid fishing with worms. The top tray was filled with a menagerie of jigs, spinners, and minnow patterns, none so large I couldn't throw it with my 6-weight. But then Nole lifted out the top tray and revealed the day's fare. "Oh," I said, looking down at the patterns. "I had a trout that size for dinner not too long ago."

Nole held up a Clouser minnow he had tied the night before: It had gleaming metal eyes and was tied with long, shiny black and white feathers. Complemented with a thick lock of sparkly synthetic, the minnow appeared ample and would surely denote a rich source of calories. "Now look under the hood," Nole said, turning the streamer on its back. Hidden by the feathers was a chemically sharpened, saltwater hook. "Point taken." Nole winked at me and laid the Clouser in my hand and stuck one other in my vest.

As I waited for Nole and Derek to finish rigging up, I watched the river flow into the western horizon. I was struck by the mood of the water and the landscape, and by how much the Bear differed from the other places I had fished in my life. How to describe the fecund emptiness? The ringing hush? The inexplicable presence of history, lingering in the afterlight of the April moon?

I remind myself that this is only a small part of the bigger picture, a five hundred yard stretch of a river that is five hundred miles long. And yet the Uinta Mountains—the headwaters of the Bear—can't be more than seventy miles east of this stretch, the last before the river empties into the Bear River Bay. Flowing through Utah, Wyoming, Idaho, and then back into Utah, one might say the Bear isn't in any hurry to get home. My kind of river.

Derek locked the van and the three of us set out. Our destination was the mouth of the Bear. Although I could not see the mouth, I could hear it. I kept watching the river for sign. Not a single rise or boil. I must admit I was skeptical: The Bear is the color of the dirt road we had taken to get here. How could anything see well enough to hunt in this water? Again, my experience on trout rivers simply hadn't prepared me for this. I had become *salmo*-centric.

The mouth of the Bear erupted to the north, where it then slammed into the earth before making a hard left to the west. The banks were high and sheer from erosion, and a thorny tangle of trees had slipped into the water, separating the things of the earth from the denizens of the Bear. Not that I had an overwhelming desire to join the river. In fact, although we were a good twenty feet away, I kept checking my distance lest I forget my place and end up in the drink.

I wondered how we were going to fish this river. I had pondered this question before on the Green and Colorado rivers. The difference is that these are big waters, rivers where anglers more or less need a boat to access the best fishing. The Bear isn't big water, but what this stretch lacks in size it makes up for in muscle. "A lot of water moving through here," I said to no one.

The sun hadn't climbed much and the milky yellow light was still a long way from the river. The water was black where it flowed beneath the banks and I imagined the drama beneath the surface. Lost in reverie, I didn't realize Derek and Nole had moved on until I saw them walking high above the river. I pulled up my collar against the chill and looked out across the refuge: Birds on the move; the wetlands faintly illuminated in the April haze of fog and pollen. Even if I could not feel it, the light looked warm and my spirits rose.

When I finally caught up to Nole, Derek had already made his way down to the water. "Did you hear that?" Nole asked. "What?" I replied, looking around. "Wipers," he said, "Let's go." I imagined a wiper holding in the dark current, a silver thread of bubbles rising from its gills. Inside each bubble is a name. One of them is mine. The names break into flight at the surface. Perhaps mine alights on a leaf to dry its wings, or maybe a swallow takes it. It occurs to me that my days on the water are filled with such reflections.

Through the trees I could see Derek stripping line on the seam of the fast and backwater, a fishing torso. "He's in deep," Nole said, sliding down the muddy bank to the river's edge. "That he is," I mumbled. Nole took a few flies from his vest and hung it from the branch of a tree before carefully stepping into the water.

The backwater was murky and blanketed with long-downed cattails that transformed the surface into a floating floor. When I contemplated the depth of the river, the heavy whispering sound of the water, and the unfamiliar power of the Bear, I realized I was out of my element. Although part of me wanted to ignore these concerns, I decided to sit on the bank and watch for a while. Nole and Derek had put some distance between them. Derek was obscured by a patch of willows, but I could clearly see Nole make his first cast. I have fly fished for only a decade, and so just about every time I watch other anglers I learn something. Or perhaps it is not so much a matter of learning as it of witnessing, in this case, skill attained through years of practice. Of course it didn't hurt that Nole had recently perfected the double-haul, which he used to precision-launch his streamer fifteen yards up and across the river.

After paying out line and letting the streamer sink, Nole began to strip in quick bursts and twitches in an effort to imitate the swan song of an ailing fish. Out of the corner of my eye I saw a spin-fisher in knee-high rubber boots and suspenders watching us from across the river. *What is he going to do in that getup?* I wondered. Then I heard Nole shout and I looked and saw that his 8-weight appeared on the verge of snapping.

"First cast!" he yelled. Derek was a few yards down river, but when he heard the commotion he appeared from behind the willows with net in hand and urged Nole to work the wiper toward him. Nole managed to coax the fish into the slow water. I'm guessing it was at that very moment that the fish saw Derek's legs and decided he had seen enough. "He's gonna run!" Derek shouted. Sure enough, the wiper surged straight into the current and then bolted down river.

I could see Nole's line buck droplets and throw spray as it peeled off the reel. A moment later he and the fish entered the standoff stage of their relationship. "He's gearing up," Derek warned. "Maybe not," Nole replied, testing the fish by slightly raising his rod. When it was clear the wiper didn't have any runs left in him, Nole used the reel-and-wait technique until he could finally net the fish. I couldn't see well from my position on the bank, but Nole and Derek were convinced they were looking at a state record.

Record or not, suddenly my apprehensions seemed as insignificant as farts in a tornado. Down the bank I went. I stuffed my net in the front of my waders and stepped into the river. I felt the earth sliding and settling so I stopped and looked around. The spin-fisher had scrambled down the bank and was standing behind the tangle. For a moment I thought he knew something we didn't, but then he cast right into the trees and I knew better.

By the time I reached the seam, the water was just below my armpits and I had acquired a golden sash of cattails. Nole saw me coming and slogged up river. "That's the honey hole, honey," he said. "Cast up the seam. Count to ten. Then strip." I peeled off some line and began working my streamer into the water. I had fished streamers once or twice in my life and without success. Therefore, and despite the fact Nole had made it look so easy, I wasn't expecting much. But after about the fifth cast I managed to find a nice line.

On either side of me the cattails formed dense patches and I could see the frost on their stalks. I cupped water in my hand and was pleased that I had worn neoprene instead of breathable waders. Once I was sure my streamer had sunk deep into the river, I pinched the line between my thumb and index finger and gave it three quick twitches. Then I paused for a couple of seconds before giving the line two more twitches and a final tug to imitate the throes of a dying fish.

Translating the death dance of another creature takes concentration. As if that weren't demanding enough, heavy swells rolled through the backwater and lifted me as if I were standing in the ocean. Somehow I managed to stay focused. But then, just as I was about to pick up my line and roll it forward, I hooked the world.

"Whatcha got on? Stickfish? Davy Jones's locker?" Nole laughed. I wasn't sure myself so I kept up my rod tip and waited. Nothing happened. I was certain I had hooked a floating log and was about to perform my own ceremony of swearing when the world on the end of my line began to swim away. "Oh, my!" I yelled. "What do we have here?" I was caught off guard by the fish's power. I had landed my share of three- to four-pound trout, but whatever was bulldogging its way out into the river felt twice as heavy as any trout I had caught.

"He's really putting his shoulder into it," I said as the wiper tugged farther and farther away. I thought of asking Nole for advice but he had since hooked up himself and was busy keeping his fish from entering the willows. My own wiper was now holding just inside the fast water. Although he was fighting both the current and me, he must have held there for a good three minutes before finally succumbing to the strain. Even then he swirled around and around in front of me, his two heavy-spined dorsal fins raised in an impressive defense.

Eventually the wiper tired and I lifted him just high enough so I could slip the hook from his mouth. I still had to be mindful of the dorsals, but after a brief struggle with the hook, I freed it and he darted back into the fast, murky water. I never laid a hand on him. I suddenly became aware of the blood pulsing in my neck and of how tired and elated I felt. Then the elation was replaced by something more akin to longing: It all happened so fast, and I was so concerned with getting the wiper back into the water, that I didn't take time to admire this unique species. I wanted another chance.

However tempted I am to think of fishing as a metaphor for life, I don't force it, if only because fishing offers so many chances to get things right. In the end, I got my chance; six of them, in fact. That's one more chance than Nole got and five more chances than Derek. Things could have just as easily turned out differently for the new guy. But by the time we left in the early afternoon, I had caught six wipers with the sun in my eyes, an empty stomach, and a bladder full of coffee. Didn't matter. I am never more alive than when hunting water. As we drove out of there I turned in my seat and watched the river flow west through the yellow fields. Like a child, I made Nole promise we would come back next April. Then I leaned back and imagined passing the time through yearlong sleep.

Confessions of a Fly Fisher

I am no stranger to the writhing worm. When I was five years old my grandfather took me bait fishing on the Snake River. He was an unabashed dangler of the worm, a brother of the dangle. Still, I never saw the man catch a trout he didn't eat. Or I should say, that we—the members of his family—didn't devour. A few nights ago I thought of him as I prepared the evening meal for Kim and our two-year-old son Wilder.

As the great Italian cook Lydia Bastianich once said, the key to the enjoyment of food is to exalt and harmonize the ingredients, which my grandfather had somehow done with a cast-iron pan, salt, pepper, butter, and flour. Of course I knew I would never be able to recreate the precise pleasure of eating my first trout, but this fish wasn't about me. It was about Kim and Wilder. Thus I felt a strong sense of responsibility to both the trout and to the people eating it. Just as my grandfather had done over a quarter century ago, I—albeit with a fly rod—had caught, killed, and served an animal I love to people I love.

However important it was for me to follow these trout on their journeys from river to pan, as a child I wasn't doing the catching and the killing. And even if I had caught and killed the trout, I doubt I would have thought beyond the initial emotions of excitement and disgust. At this stage in my life, however, I try to think past first responses in an attempt to better understand the experience of fishing, which is also a way to better understand myself.

Fly fishing and bait fishing are undoubtedly similar in some respects, but each activity seems to awaken and call upon different parts of our nature. It is one thing to tie on a delicate imitation of a grasshopper made from thread and feathers. It is quite another to disembowel a worm or to impale some other living thing for the sake of catching prey. Ultimately, it is a short cast from fly fishing—the art of dabbling with killing—to bait fishing—the art of actually killing. I think this is one of the reasons why my friend Bert Bender—the embodiment of bait fishing and so much else—has always been so interesting to me, and why I was therefore quick to accept his offer to go night fishing for flathead catfish. I'm not sure it is even possible to fly fish for catfish. They live at great depths and eat only living bait. And Bert wasn't going after just any flathead. Rather, he was after the forty- to sixty-pound behemoths that patrolled the deepest parts of Bartlett Lake. When it comes to fishing, Bert is a natural born killer. But he is also quite possibly the gentlest man I have ever known.

Until recently, Bert was a professor of American literature. Throughout his tenure at the university, at the end of each school year he would head for Alaska, where he worked as a small-scale commercial fisherman. Bert had spent thirty summers plying the frigid waters of Cook's Inlet before finally selling his boat and calling it quits. Based on what he's told me, the work is bloody, brutal, and dangerous. Fishing for flathead isn't exactly dangerous, but it would still give me a chance to experience this form of fishing and to learn from an expert.

Bartlett Lake is about forty-five minutes northeast of Phoenix. The travel was easy going until we left the freeway. The road rolled and curved through untouched desert. But that wasn't my biggest problem. "Pip," Bert's fourteen-foot, fold-up boat, runs on a little gas-powered engine. Bert hadn't closed the vents on the gas can, so by the time we reached the lake, the fumes had taken their toll. Right when we pulled up, I stepped out into the barreling dust and vomited. Bert was unaffected. Perhaps he had developed immunity from his years on the water. Or was it that his sniffer had gone to pot? Either way, it didn't bother him.

As a fly fisher, my primary mode of transportation is walking. Thus I have always prided myself on using my own steam to get from point A to point T. I reminded myself of this fact but I still felt a little embarrassed by my weak stomach. *What next?* I wondered. *Seasickness on the fucking lake?* Though hot and damp with evaporation, the desert air was a welcome change. I looked down at Bartlett. The water was smooth and still, except for rises in the shallows, like a light rain. The ever-widening circles meant the bluegills were feeding. Bert had loosened all the ties to the boat and was now watching the lake. "Good," he said.

We lifted off the boat and carried it to the end of the ramp. Balls of gnats undulated above the water. Easy pickings for the dragon flies and swallows that flitted and careened in the dissolving light. "How are you feeling?" "Better," I said. "Hell of a way to start a trip." "Tell me about it." In truth I still felt clammy and unsteady, but Bert is such a tough old guy, I was inspired to ignore my discomfort. We were also in a beautiful place. So rather than focusing on my inner turmoil, I swallowed hard and tried to focus on my surroundings.

As I walked back to the jeep for the motor, I could smell creosote mixed with the tangy stench of a javelina carcass that had been dragged onto the boat ramp and picked clean. I toed the carcass to get a better look at the huge canines and perhaps detect some sign—a bullet hole, broken bones, something—that might explain the death. I didn't get too far into my speculations before a brightly spotted whiptail lizard ran into view and climbed up a boulder, perhaps to eyeball me and to bask in the final moments of sunlight. In the western distance, long gauzy clouds appeared soaked in flame. Standing there with the carcass, whiptail, and all that sky, I had to wonder how I fit into this world and into the equation beyond the blaze.

The motor weighed a good fifty pounds. I hugged it to my body like something precious and carried it down to the lake. After three trips, Bert and I had readied the boat and loaded it with the night's provisions. The sun was gone from view and the light was quickly withdrawing into the west. Not long before total dark. "We've got a few minutes," Bert said, smoothing his beard. "Let's get some bait." He waded out to the stern and grabbed a white bucket then waded back to shore.

"Toss me that bag, will you?" I leaned into the boat and pulled out the bag. Bert unzipped it and produced two coils of line. Each coil terminated in a hook as fine as an eyelash. For the moment, Bert was all business. I admired the desert, which lay awash in reddish light. "What a sight," I said. Bert looked up. The embers in the west burned in his glasses. "Yes, it is," he said musingly and as though he had just eaten something delicious.

We launched the boat in full dark. The white wake curled away as we motored to the center of the lake. No moon. Millions of stars. "Take this," Bert called above the motor. I switched on the spotting lamp and used it to light up the shore and then scan what lay ahead in the darkness. The grebes parted before us as if members of an aquatic procession. "We're OK here, Max. Our eyes will adjust." "Aye aye, Cap'n," I said, switching off the light. "Where are we going?" I asked. Bert eased off the throttle until the little four-stroke purred. "I've got a couple spots in mind."

I swiveled around and kept my eyes ahead. The boat was moving faster now and I could not keep up with the shapes that formed out there in the darkness. I looked back at Bert and wondered how he could be so sure we would not collide with some wreckage hidden out there in the night. After a few minutes of this vigilance, I was exhausted. I was about to break rank and turn on the spotting lamp. *The hell with it*, I thought. Then Bert cut the motor and the boat slogged to a halt before the wake of our sudden inertia set us forward.

Several buoy posts and then shore came into view. The posts were gray and barren, like the remains of a nuclear forest. On one of them a ghostly blue heron stood on one foot, its beak folded into a robe of blue-gray feathers. Its eyes open and unmoving. "Anchor's in the bow there," Bert said. I felt around and found the anchor and then hoisted it over the gunwale. The rope was a hundred feet and the anchor took forty of it before resting on the lake floor. Bert suggested I drag the anchor until I could feel it catch bottom. I did so, then I tied off the line and looked at the thick stars in the limitless dark.

Bert pieced together what he called his elephant gun, a heavy-duty rod designed to bring in the bruisers of the deep. He fed the thick, snow-blue line through the eyelets and added a big metal weight. I considered commenting on the crudeness of the gear, but luckily I caught myself before I could grossly miss the point. Every now and then a breeze would blow in from the desert and chill the sweat on my forehead. As I looked around, I realized my eyes had adjusted and that I could now see Bert surprisingly well. He pulled up the white bucket and placed it between his feet. "Hmmm," he said, peering into the bucket. "We've got Condi, Dick, Rummy, Rove, and Dubya. Whom should we send in first?"

Including the members of the Bush administration, there were actually a dozen bluegills in the water. They had arranged themselves in a wheel and were facing the bucket. Looking at them, I remembered a Kauai rancher telling me her horses would come in from the pasture and face the barn long before a hurricane made landfall. I thought about this and about the importance of watching other animals. What can they tell us? What might we tell them? And how much of our own animal awareness had been lost or lay dormant?

Bert reached into the water and grabbed one of the fish. He was careful to avoid the dorsal, which was now raised in protest. "Sorry, little fella." The bluegill bowed and stiffened as Bert slid the hook between its spine and dorsal. "Catch us a big one," he said as he brought back the rod and pushed it forward. The line spiraled through the eyelets and then made a *whump* when the weight hit the water. Bert rested the rod against the gunwale so that the tip was silhouetted against the horizon. "Now we see who comes calling."

I imagined the bluegill being dragged down into the cold darkness. In my mind I could see the weight hit bottom, the silt rising and falling around it. At first the bluegill is disoriented. Then it attempts to swim away and instead swims round and round: a sentence in hell for those who believe in such things. I don't know what the fish knows, but common sense suggests that it knew things weren't going well. Bluegills aren't defenseless, however: Apart from the spiny dorsal, they have large mock eyes just behind their gill plates that have some interesting defensive functions.

For starters the false eyes distract predators away from the bluegill's brain and sense organs in the event of an attack. The mock eyes are also significantly larger than the bluegill's true eyes and therefore denote a much larger fish, which may discourage predators from attacking in the first place. But any defense is effective only to a certain point. Against a large flathead, a fish that is anywhere from twenty to a hundred times bigger than the bluegill swimming on the end of Bert's line, such defenses are futile.

The far-off howl of a coyote ended the quiet spell. Then another coyote called back. "He's really close," I whispered. Bert took out a mason jar of red wine and drank. "You could fish that hand line," he said, handing me the jar. I was content to just sit there, drink Bert's wine, and enjoy the strangeness of the night. However, the angler in me also knew that another line in the water meant another shot at catching a flathead. Bacchus was calling, but I decided I couldn't sit there and let that line go to waste.

I looked into the bucket and saw the dark backs of the bluegills. Perhaps sensing my reluctance, Bert shined a small flashlight. "What about that one there?" Before I could answer he reached down and snatched one up. I was fine with that because it saved me the trouble of asking him to hook it for me. I knew that it had to be done just so or the bluegill would be immobilized. Once Bert had hooked the fish he eased the rig into the water. "OK, go ahead, let out the line." I peeled off about forty feet of line before the weight would take no more. Then I laid the spool on the floor and returned to my night vigil.

Shore was not far off and I could hear small waves lapping the sand and gravel. Every now and then a gnat would whine in my ear or something—a fish or bird?—would splash out there in the dark. The desert sounds together with our own were oddly emphatic in the vacuum of silence. "You have something?" Bert asked. "I don't know." Drifting in and out of the moment, I hadn't seen my line sliding along the gunwale. I picked up the line and felt the faint yet unmistakable life force of a fish.

How many times had I lifted some fish from the darkness? Thousands, surely. And yet the experience retains all its fullness. "Are you sure you've got a fish?" Bert asked. "Either that or an old boot," I said, recoiling the line as I hoisted the fish toward the boat. I could tell this fish was no forty-pounder, however. It wasn't even a five-pounder. In fact, subtract the organs, skin, and bones and not a pound of flesh was edible.

As I worked to release what turned out to be a three-pound catfish, I noticed purple blood vessels spreading like a delicate root system across the white-gray pigment of its body. Clearly this creature did not dwell in the sunlight. The hook made a hollow popping sound when I finally freed it from the fish's mouth. Instead of swimming away, the fish sank. I shined the light into the water. Still sinking. "Revive, you bastard." Then the fish spiraled out of sight. I cupped some lake water in my hand. *Bon appetite*.

We sat on that spot for a good forty-five minutes without hooking into another fish. I was feeling a bit antsy, so when Bert reeled in to check his bait, I asked if he would ferry me to shore. "Good idea," he said. "Stretch your legs for a bit." He steered the boat into a cove and reduced the speed. I could see a sandy bank and he put Pip ashore. "I'll see you in a few," I said, pushing the boat back into the water. Bert rowed about twenty yards to the mouth of the cove and went to work re-rigging his line.

In my haste, I had forgotten to bring a light, without which I wasn't going far. Apart from the dangers of the terrain, including several species of cacti, this was the hour of the rattlesnake. I had lived in the Sonora Desert long enough to have encountered my share of rattlers, including Mojave and Western Diamondbacks. Over the years I had learned to predict their behavior and to anticipate their whereabouts . . . during the day. But at night the snakes are on the move, in which case my knowledge was next to useless.

I kept my eyes on the ground and my ears wide open as I walked a little ways inland. I found a small hill of rock from which I scanned the cove and the surrounding area. Bert and the boat had merged into a single mass of noiseless black. Against this silence, a small rockslide on the other side of the cove sounded like an epic event. I knew it could have been caused by any number of animals, including deer, javelina, coyote, mountain lion, or even a young black bear, which are often displaced by larger bears during the driest parts of the year.

I walked quietly down the hill until I reached the shore opposite the side where the slide had occurred. The sandy shoreline was illuminated with starlight. Though faint, it was enough to articulate the outline of a javelina that had come down for a drink. I whispered loudly to Bert but he didn't hear me until I finally called his name outright, at which point I was sure that the javelina would flee. But the javelina went on unperturbed. What an unexpected pleasure, watching and listening to another animal drink.

Without the moon for reference, I had no idea of the time, but I knew it had to be around midnight. The cove wasn't yielding so we decided to head up the lake to the inlet, where the Verde River had gouged a deep trough into the lake floor. Now that spring runoff had dwindled, the trough offered the flathead an excellent place to hunt. Bert assured me that this was our best chance of catching a big flathead. We were down to eight bluegills, too, which was another reason to get to the best hole and fish it for the duration.

I situated myself in the bow. Having spent the last few hours adjusting to this new environment, I loosened my grip on the lamp and let down my guard. Without the parameters imposed by the objects of my vision, I was lulled by the shapeless void. I closed my eyes and relished the inner night together with the heat from the wine and the cold bits of spray on my hands and face. This was the life.

But I wasn't completely inside myself: If I thought I saw something, I would switch on the lamp. Otherwise I relied on my night vision to detect any danger or delight we may happen upon. In the distance I could make out what appeared to be a peninsula that stretched far into the lake. It was then that I realized we had drifted from the center of the lake and had moved shoreward. I turned to ask Bert if our change of course was acceptable, but he was already standing as high as he could without letting go of the motor arm. He hadn't stood up like that all night so I knew something was wrong.

I turned back to see what I had apparently missed, but we had already run aground. I must have gripped the gunwales the moment I saw Bert standing because after the boat had stopped I had hardly moved. I switched on the lamp and shined it into the water: We had hit a hidden shoal. The motor was still running and the sand swirled in the greenish water. "Hang on," Bert said as he put the motor into reverse and gunned it. Once we were off the shoal, Bert rocked the motor out of the water and examined the propeller. A couple of new chinks in the blades, but no serious damage. That's sort of how I felt, too.

We got back to the boat ramp just as the sun was rising. I washed my face in the lake and looked across the sleeping desert. The inimitable richness of life lies in the enjoyment of small things: drinking wine, baiting hooks, facing the setting sun, and confronting darkness. But now the sunlight slipped across the canyon walls. Apart from a pair of sandpipers picking tiny invertebrates from the mud, the world was still and silent; as if for those moments it were listening for something so faint, if I breathed I would not hear it.

Decision
Water

I cast my first fly during the summer of 1994. I am sure of the year because I had just left Utah to attend graduate school in Arizona. That first summer and several after it, I would close my books, pack up my '71 VW Bug, and head back to Utah. Sometimes I'd stay for two weeks; other times I'd stay for two months. Predictably, the longer I'd stay, the harder it was to leave. The old story. It took me several years before I could let go and enjoy the Arizona wilderness and the waters I found there. Of course I never did let go completely, but enough to where Utah rivers weren't always on my mind.

If dreams are an indication, I was utterly obsessed with fly fishing. Several nights a week I would wet my line in dream water. Some dreams were of familiar locations and seemed fairly literal (sometimes a wet line is just a wet line). Other dreams were more symbolic and featured exotic destinations. As tellingly, perhaps, is that even now in my waking life I will see flowing water, say, in a moss-lined gutter after a rain, and I will look for trout in it. However devoted I was to the art, I became competent only after three years of fly fishing, which was about the same time it took to complete graduate school. I guess that makes me a double major.

Call it luck or, as Norman Maclean's father did, disgracing the fish, but despite my neophyte status and at times questionable tactics, I caught trout my first day out and on pretty much all the days that followed. That's one of the seductive things about fly fishing: It can be done poorly and still be effective. It is sort of like life in that regard: On a very basic level, one doesn't have to be all that good at it to live it. That said, I'm not proud of foul-hooked eyes and hook-torn abdomens, nor of my own foul moods when the river hasn't gone my way. They give me pause. But what can I do except try to live by an improved perspective, an ever-growing confection of humility, wisdom, and perhaps a trace of embarrassment and shame?

When it comes to remembering, a little shame goes a long way: How easily I recall my fly fishing follies. Naturally, my first season was by far the most folly-laden. I would have my share of misadventure in Arizona (suspecting my rod tip was broken, I bent it back and forth and broke it myself), but the most important incidents took place in Utah on the Provo River. That first year I would fish the Weber River a good deal and would also make the occasional trip east to the Duchesne and Strawberry Rivers, but I cut my teeth on the middle section of the Provo. At that time, I doubt a body could find a prettier stretch of river.

Years ago, the middle Provo was unparalleled in terms of overall appeal, largely because until recently the section remained unknown to most anglers. If the Provo came up at all, it was the much-lauded and greatly pressured lower section. As a result, the middle was left intact. I might have found some beer bottles strewn around a bucket once or twice where some yokel spent the lunch hour. Otherwise, encountering signs of other humans was unusual. When I walked into the trees along the river and would see a great horned owl, or hear a song sparrow, or glimpse a browsing deer and the flash of a red-tail fox, I felt like an unlikely visitor.

The middle has pastureland on either side, and it is therefore not uncommon to bushwhack one's way right into a herd of steers; an unnerving experience, to be sure. Much of this land remains even now, although increasingly parcels have been put up for sale and the so-called McMansions have begun to appear along the river's edge, especially where it runs near Midway, a little town that for many years was part of what made fishing the middle section so special. What was once a small country town has since modernized and lost some of its rural charm. But I'd like to think I haunted the town in its heyday, when a two-lane road ran through the middle of it. A country road is certainly one of the small pleasures in life, but it is doubly so when it leads to a meal.

Named after the neighboring Timpanogos Mountains, the Timpfreeze Diner featured a pinball machine, thick homemade shakes, and cheeseburgers wrapped in yellow wax paper. After a full day on the river, someone would ask, "Are you thinking what I'm thinking?" At that time I did most of my fishing with my friend Nole, who was eager to try his luck and agree that whoever caught the next trout wouldn't have to buy lunch. We both did our share of losing this traditional bet, although as I write Nole still owes me two meals. That they will be taken at Timpfreeze seems doubtful, however. Since the town began the process of modernization—an aspect of which is widening the road to four lanes—the old gal who owns the place hasn't bothered opening. Maybe the juggernaut of progress will slow and she'll open her doors again. Otherwise it's braving hotdogs at the gas station.

I remember one evening many years ago when Nole and I stopped to get some gas and a hotdog for the drive back to Salt Lake. Nole had lost the day's bet and so while he was inside rounding up some grub, I sat in the car and relaxed. We had fished from dawn to dusk and the fishing had been excellent. Not wanting to miss a moment of the action, I didn't put down my rod all day. After this marathon, I was giddy with excitement, thirst, and hunger. Then an old Ford pulled in beside us and the passenger went inside. The driver, who was perhaps a few years older than me and about a foot higher off the ground, glanced into the back of Nole's car and asked me how we did.

Pleased by his interest, I sat up and, with some measure of restraint, told him we had done really well. "We slayed 'em," I said, trying out some of the lingo I had learned. He turned a little in his seat and his face got real thoughtful. "Oh, yeah," he said, "what were you using? Streamers?" At that time I didn't even know what a streamer was. But I didn't want the guy to think I was a beginner (which is of course exactly what I was), so I quickly took a mental inventory of the flies we had used and found the one that had attracted the most interest. "Nah," I blurted, "Chunk-a-meat."

The guy looked around as if to make sure no one were listening. Clearly he was uncomfortable, but why? For a second I thought he was going to try and sell me some drugs. "OK, well, you don't want to be telling anybody that," he said in that way that meant this was just between us. "Were you guys above the bridge?" I said we were. "Yeah, well, that section's got special regs. No bait, Hoss." *Regs? Bait? Hoss? What the hell is he talking about?* Just then the guy's buddy walked out with a case of beer and climbed into the truck. "You take it easy," the driver said.

As they pulled away, I took a long drink of water and processed our exchange. *Oh, shit,* I thought. The guy had taken me *literally*. In my euphoria—my stupor, really—I assumed he had heard of the chunk. And why wouldn't I have? I could refer to the equally bizarre-sounding hare's ear and anglers seemed to know what I meant. What made the chunk so special? As is so often true, the answer is in the question. I didn't know it then, but the chunk is Nole's creation, in which case probably a dozen people on the planet knew that the chunk *is* actually a fly. When Nole got in the car I told him what happened and we both laughed. Suddenly *I* was Hoss the yokel, fishing with big ugly hooks and cubes of meat. *You schmuck,* I said to myself.

Had this fellow been with Fish and Game or the FFABF (Fly Fishers Against Bait Fishing), I would have had some explaining to do. But apart from the embarrassment of misspeaking, that was probably as bad as it was going to get. Thus it is with an entirely different feeling that I recall other times when, under the quasi-narcotic influence of angling, I made some seriously unwise decisions. One particular chain of unfortunate events started with my refusal—of all things—to use a strike indicator, which resulted in a lot of guesswork and, presumably, lost fish. But I didn't care. I had caught fish without the indicator, so when Nole urged me to use one I asked him why I should fix what wasn't broken.

We were fishing the upper Provo where it feeds Jordanelle reservoir. The water was running high and had created several small islands. I figured I could pick my way along the islands until I reached the mouth of the river, which was thick with spawning rainbows. Spring runoff may last well into July provided the mountains got lots of snowfall. Under these conditions, the air temperature could be a balmy eighty-five degrees but the water wouldn't be half that warm. This was one of those days. What I really needed, then, was a pair of chest waders to keep the cold mountain water at bay. Under the self-cast spell of the fly rod, I threw out caution and, with nothing but a pair of hip boots, shorts, and a light shirt, made the thirty-yard slog to the mouth of the river.

The islands turned out to be little more than patches of high grass and therefore offered only psychological reprieves from the frigid water. But I was hell-bent on connecting with these bejeweled slivers of living river, so on I went. I made my stand on the tip of the outermost patch of grass where, if I stood just so, the water would not spill into my boots. For a while there all was well: Even without an indicator, I managed to catch three or four fat trout in quick succession, all on the retrieve. Maintaining my position was not easy, however, and with so little room for error, it wasn't long before my hip boots had filled with the cold water.

Once that happened, I had to make a choice: Stay put, go back, or walk farther out into the water. Given my casting limitations, I decided to keep walking. Eventually I came to the river's edge. Until now I could look down into the water and see the flooded earth. Here there was nothing but black. I must have shivered in that water for a good two hours, but I was standing in a beautiful river on a warm spring evening catching fish. Within the first hour, I had thought of getting out, but I was entranced. Listening to the killjoy known as my body was therefore out of the question. This all changed, however, the moment my thoughts started stumbling into each other as if I were drunk: I knew I had to get out of the water, fast.

Various species of turtle instinctively head for the sea the instant they hatch and climb out of their nests of sand. Having left the sea long ago, my own encoding directed me toward land. Trouble is, I had wandered out some forty yards. Although I knew better, initially I went from island to island, hoping to find one that truly was above water. Finding them as I left them, with twenty-five yards to go, I made a beeline for shore. When I got there, Nole had already broken down his rod and put away his gear. Of course he was bone dry.

"Are you OK?" he asked. I didn't answer him. Fearing the onset of hypothermia, I had to get moving. After I had kicked off my hip boots, and the water and a couple of trout had come gushing out, I took a brisk walk up the road. I made like a windmill with my arms and lifted each knee to my chest as I walked. It must have been a pathetic sight. But I kept on and didn't go back until I started feeling warm. When I finally did get back to the car, Nole was sitting on the hood enjoying the last rays of sunlight. "I never wondered what the karate kid would look like on speed," he said, smiling with his eyes closed. "Oh, yeah?" I asked. "Yeah," he said, "but thanks to you, now I know."

Although not without its humor, the experience changed how I look at the river. I should probably be thankful. For if I had to have the experience and learn the hard way (and obviously I didn't), it was better to do so sooner than later. Once I knew this particular expression of cold, I could properly prepare for it. At least that was the argument I made one summer morning when I showed up at Nole's fully outfitted in my neoprene chest waders and felt-soled boots. "You're going to get major swamp ass," he said, reminding me we had an hour-and-a-half drive ahead of us. "Maybe so," I said, "maybe so." But he was right: I had overdone it. It's all about finding a balance.

However much I would like to believe that balance is a state of mind, a sort of enlightened orientation that, once attained, touches all aspects of one's life, that hasn't been my experience. Of course I do not dispute the relationship between one's mental foothold in life and one's physical foothold. Still, finding balance in one thing is not necessarily finding balance in another. One of the last times I fished the middle section was in the late spring of 2006, which is when Kim and our son Wilder and I moved back to Salt Lake. We hadn't been in town for more than a month when I finally found some time to visit my old friend, the middle Provo.

During the twelve years I had lived in Arizona, I had fished several rivers and just about every lake in the White Mountains. But as anglers know, rivers and lakes make very different demands. In the past when I would visit Utah and Nole and I would go fishing, I would tell him that lake fishing had made me soft. What I really meant was that I needed some time to refamiliarize myself with the river environment. Usually it didn't take long. I don't know how many summers I would return to the middle section and find the same river I had left a year ago. Same holes, same runs with only modest changes. Maybe a beaver had felled one of the many trees under which I sat to get out of the sun, or perhaps the steers had articulated a new path through the brush. Otherwise the semiotics of the river had remained somewhat constant.

On this last trip, however, it was as though I had walked into a familiar house and found a stranger sitting in my chair. I recognized much of what

I saw, but the mood of the river had changed and so had the volume. The old crossings were gone and, like the road through Midway, the river had grown to three times its normal size. My friend Morley would call this "decision water." Although used to describe that split second when the fly enters the trout's field of vision and the fish must decide whether to take what is proffered, the phrase also refers to the moment when an angler must decide if he should take a risk and, in this case, attempt to cross the river.

Finding the first crossing under three feet of fast-moving water, I walked until I came to a place where the river broke into three braids and thus distributed the flow. A bank of clouds moved across the sun and the river bottom appeared very dark. As the clouds moved off, the sunlight returned to the water and I could see all but the last few yards of bottom. I was wearing breathable chest waders, but I knew they wouldn't necessarily protect me if I went down. How many times had I heard of anglers who had been dragged under after they had fallen and their chest waders had filled with water? As dangerous, perhaps, was that I was wearing hiking boots instead of felt-soled boots. Not an ideal situation. I therefore took my time studying the water and planning my route. Then I stepped into the fluid muscle.

Once I got to the other side, I looked up river, hoping to see if not a good, then at least a fishable, line. I couldn't see far and what I did see looked more rapid than river. The high water had overtaken the path and spread far into the trees and bushes. Apart from going back the way I came, I either had to bushwhack or scramble up a steep bank and then walk high above the water. I would have a better view from above so I climbed the bank. When I got to the top I was a sweaty mess and the flies found me delightful. I tipped back my hat and wiped the sweat from my forehead. I could see a half-mile or so, to the point where the river banked to the east and out of view. That half-mile didn't look good. But I knew there were a couple of spots around the corner where the river again broke into several channels.

I hadn't done much river fishing for over a year, which is why I think I gave the middle a chance. If I were to pull up and see the same river today, I would have left my rod in the car and gone birding. Instead, I remained cautiously optimistic and set out across the ridge. Having read my fair share of American literature, I often think about protagonists whose trials and tribulations mirror my own. The protagonist in Jack London's story *To Build a Fire* makes an ill-fated decision to trek across the Alaskan wilderness in winter. London implies that had the character been more attentive to natural language and heeded its warnings, he might have made it out alive.

The high water should have been the only warning I needed, but it wasn't until I saw an uprooted tree barreling down the river that I realized the extent of the danger. By then I had walked a mile in the hot sun and was running low on enthusiasm. Once I finally accepted the fact that there would be no fishing today, my focus shifted to getting back across the river. The obvious solution was to walk back to where I had crossed originally, but the sun and terrain had taken a toll on my energy. I knew there was a wide and shallow riffle up ahead, so instead of turning back, I worked my way to the river.

The riffle of my memory had been replaced with an unbroken sheet of golden water. I used to call this run Christmas Tree because there was a downed Russian olive tree at the top of it that was adorned with many of my flies. Now the run as I knew it was gone. I watched the water flow past my feet and marveled at the greenish-gold color of the stones. The moment I stepped into the river I knew I was in trouble. But I had no choice except to keep going. Perhaps that's another aspect of decision water: Once a decision is made, there is no turning back.

The water came to the middle of my thighs and was moving with such speed that for each step I took across the river, I was carried six steps down and closer to the end of the run. There the river narrowed into a trough of deep water that swelled and rolled with rapids the size of barrels. But the river also carried me slantwise, in which case I had made it about halfway across in only three steps. I had fifteen feet to go. *I can do this*, I thought. Then I thought *Oh, you dumb shit* just as I felt myself going down.

I was holding my rod in my right hand and so I went down on my left. I felt a sharp pain in my left hand and knee as the water broke over my shoulder and into my shirt. My feet slid beneath me as if I were on ice. At no time did I have more than one hand or foot in contact with the river bottom. I rose and fell, rose and fell, and each time I would drive my hand into the stones and push myself up, clawing, gasping, and hoping for a lasting foothold in the world. The golden river water washed down my insides and flooded my ears with the gurgling sound of words spoken beneath the water. I could smell the river slime and see the muted earth as the water moved over me and the air escaped from unseen insects. I shut my eyes and clawed.

When I opened them again it was to the hard and unchanged sunlight. I crawled out of the shallows and stood up. My hand did not appear broken, so although it throbbed, I concentrated on checking my knee. As I unsnapped my chest-waders, I checked my Swarovski optics for damage. Much to my surprise, apart from a few drops of water, they were fine. But that wasn't my only spell of luck: Although my shirt was soaked from sleeve to collar, my chest waders hadn't taken on more than a half-cup of water. These facts alone seemed improbable, but once I realized I didn't drop or break my rod—or even lose my hat, for that matter—I began to suspect that I had stumbled on the omega fact, the fact-at-the-end-of-all-facts, and that I was, in fact, dead.

I knew I was being ridiculous, but just in case, I went through a corporeal checklist that culminated in a big drink of water and a hearty burp. For one thing I could taste river. For another I figured that belching would be entirely gratuitous in any afterlife-like setting. I was shivering so I closed my eyes and turned to the sun. I imagined Search and Rescue pulling my body from the river. My rod, hat, and one of my boots are gone. In fact, if it weren't for that bare left foot poking up out of the water, the men doubt they would have found me as quickly as they did. I know this because I can hear the two of them talking as they load me into the truck. I am back there with some rope, a pick, and a round-nose shovel. Good company. The older man notices the white band of skin on my ring finger. "Ring's gone," he says. I think it will be hours before they know who I am. For me the day is over, but for them it is nearing nightfall and one of them has got to make a decision.

The Killing
Place

Three thousand feet below and partly obscured by cloud, the island's edge appeared and vanished into the Pacific. I squeezed Kim's hand as the plane banked and my stomach banked along with it. After six hours of travel, we were about to set foot on the most remote archipelagos in the world. Kim had just finished graduate school and to celebrate her achievement her parents sprang for a trip to Kauai, Hawaii. Once we arrived at our lodgings, I threw my suitcase on the bed, put on some shorts, and headed down to the beach. Within yards, the manicured grounds, swimming pool, tennis court, and rich (and mostly non-indigenous) flora opened onto the raw featurelessness of all life's birthplace, the ocean.

I gazed at the cliffs down the beach. It was still early and the sun was low on the horizon. Thus the outline of the rock and the dense vegetation that grew atop it appeared very black against the sky. Suddenly a man appeared from out of the blackness and ran toward the edge of the cliff. Then he stopped and grabbed a large fishing rod that had been propped in the rocks, and that was now bouncing like an upside-down "U." Whatever was on the end of his line was big. I sat up to get a better look. How is he going to bring that fish to hand from a hundred-fifty vertical feet in the air?

The longer I watched, the more intrigued I became. Although I could not make out the line itself, I could discern the angle of the rod tip, which I traced some thirty yards out into the ocean. Having struggled to haul trout out of the water and up a two-foot high river bank, I couldn't figure out how he was going to close the deal from that height. I scanned the base of the cliff for a fellow angler, someone to help bring in the fish. Nothing. A few minutes later, the man had worked the fish into the water just below the cliff, where it struggled and thrashed. The hook set, the man seated the rod closer to the edge of the cliff and attached a gaff to the line. Then he slid the gaff down the line and somehow worked it into the fish's mouth. Now hoisted into the sky, the fish was easy to identify: a yellowfin tuna.

Unlike the languid tuna depicted on the side of tunafish cans, the real thing is nimble, sleek, and beautiful. That is the outside: The yellowfin's flesh is one of the most delicious on the planet; a fact evinced by the precipitous decline of the fish's numbers. As I stood up to go, I wondered what it meant to fish (and eat) responsibly in the throes of such decline. I saw the fisherman move along the tuna, his right shoulder sawing as he opened and cleaned the fish. Watching him, I realized I was seeing part of the answer: one man, one fish. Just as it has been for millennia on this island.

When I got back to the condo, Kim and her parents had gone to the store, but my brother-in-law James—also the beneficiary of his parents' generosity—was sitting on the patio. Spread out on the table were several brochures with information about guided fishing trips. James had selected one and set it aside. "What's this?" I asked, picking up the brochure. "Take a look," James said. The brochure advertised fishing for the beautiful and elusive peacock bass, so-called because of its bright coloration. Accentuated by reddish-orange fins and three dark vertical slashes down its sides, the peacock appears tiger-like. Were it not for the large mock eye on its tail, the peacock bass may well have been more aptly named tiger bass. "Pretty fish." James took off his ball cap, smoothed his hair, and returned the cap to his head. "What do you think?" I looked at the brochure again. "Let's do it."

James made the reservation for the next day, so we got up early that morning and met our fishing guide at a gas station down the road. The guide showed up with a fourteen-foot skiff. The boat had seen better days, and I'm guessing so had the guide. His hair was long and loosely curled and his face had the puffy sheen of too much sun and one-too-many shots of whiskey. Short and squat, he stood a little higher than five feet and was densely muscled. I had to admit, though, that for a man in his forties, he was in good shape.

After putting some air in the sagging trailer tires, the guide told James and me to hop in and we'd get going. When the three of us were snugly seated in the cab of an old Toyota pickup, the guide introduced himself as Moondog and shook hands with the two of us. Sun-browned, rough-skinned, and knuckle-cracked: workingman's hands.

As we drove along the coast, Moondog commented on various attractions: the plantation where they filmed such-and-such a movie; the stretch of beach where a surfer was recently attacked by a shark. Then he'd point up into the hills and dreamily comment on the land he hoped to buy there someday. This went on until we finally turned onto a dirt road that ran parallel to one of the many freshwater rivers on Kauai, the source of which is rainfall and underground springs. I could hear the rods and gear sliding around in the boat as we hit potholes and negotiated deep wheel ruts made after a heavy rain. The soil was sunset red with a hint of gray and so offered a pronounced contrast to surrounding vegetation.

The brush along the river was high and dense, but every few yards it would open and I would glimpse a black bar of river, smooth and mono-lithic. Soon the brush opened up and there was a makeshift boat ramp and boardwalk made from a mishmash of boards, metal, and plastic. James and I slid out of the truck to take a look while Moondog hurriedly swung around and backed in the boat. James stood off to one side and tentatively offered directions, not because he wasn't genuinely interested in helping, but because Moondog pretty much ignored him. I looked at James and made a goofy grin. James laughed, folded his arms, and then took a step back as Moondog finally got it right.

I figured we had a few minutes so I walked a little ways up the road. Ambivalently lead on by the acrid odor of decomposition, I had made it just beyond a thicket of bush beard grass when Moondog honked the horn. But I lingered for moment, because there, unceremoniously heaped in a pile and covered in a litter of palm fronds, fast food bags, and a tattered blanket were several animals.

Obscured by refuse and each other, two of the animals were not readily identifiable, but I could clearly see a young horse lying atop the heap. He had a fissure down the center of his skull and his eyes opened onto the water. I was tempted to pull a frond over his face to keep the sun off of it, but I knew that was presumption on my part because there could have been a thousand suns above that horse and it wouldn't have made one bit of difference.

When I got back to the ramp, James and Moondog were sitting in the boat with the motor idling. "Hop in and I'll push us off." I carefully stepped into the middle of the boat and sat down. A second later I heard a loud snort. I turned around and Moondog pinched his nose on one side and exhaled violently. Farmer blow. Then he gunned the motor and we slogged out into the river, which here breached the banks and spread into the grass. The river was so smooth and quiet, I would have mistaken it for a still water had I not seen the grass bending on the river's edge.

We motored up river to a small cove where we could rig up. Moondog whistled a little song as he tied on a rubber frog for James. He whistled well, in long, full, melodious notes. And I remember thinking his little song was so far the best thing to come out of his mouth. He handed the rod to James and offered a brief explanation of how to fish the frog. Not that James needed any explanation: He'd been fishing the still waters of the South for many years and was therefore well versed in the corresponding methods. But James did the polite thing and listened attentively to what Moondog was saying.

For the moment, I was feeling beguiled by Moondog's mellifluous whistle. It reminded me of a scene from a prison movie I had seen years ago. One evening, after the lights had gone out on the cellblock, the most fearsome of all inmates—a huge bald man with a rumpled face—began singing *Down in the Valley*. He sang so beautifully that, like his fellow inmates, I was awestruck. I wanted to ask Moondog to whistle some more, but I checked that impulse for obvious reasons.

I had read that most of the plants tourists see once they get off the plane are in fact invasive, so instead I asked him about the surrounding flora. If connecting with the world stems from asking the right questions, I seemed to have hit pay dirt. Judging by how Moondog's face and body opened, I prepared myself for an earful. But as if relishing the power that comes from having a captive audience and the one true answer, Moondog refrained from answering right away. "Run this minnow right along the edge there," he said, simultaneously pointing across the river and handing me the rod. "Get down deep and then jig it up." James had already started side-arming his frog across the river and swimming it atop the water. I had never seen a frog fished before and I thought it looked like the real thing. As the moments passed I decided that invasive flora must have been a sore subject, so I flipped the bail on my reel and accidentally cast far left of my target.

"Well now . . ." Moondog said, ". . . the plants are a big problem. See all that leafy shit covering those trees?" To the untrained eye, it all looked the same: green. "Yeah," I lied. Moondog spat into the water. "That's banana poka vine. What they call 'blight.' *Blupe*. Nice cast." James had just put his frog just inside the grass and then began popping it across the river top. "That's one deceptive amphibian." When nothing happened, Moondog fumbled around for the cooler and offered us a soda. "Shasta?" James took one and cracked it. "No thanks." I turned and cast on the opposite side of the boat, waited for a few seconds, and then began reeling. I felt the lure swimming deep underwater and the tug of the current. "Try quickening your retrieve," Moondog said. "The less time they have to look at the bait, the better."

Moondog's reasoning made sense to me and I nodded in agreement. I must confess, though, that I have not always been so receptive to the wisdom of other anglers. Luckily I was far enough along in my own development that I understood the value of Moondog's experience and welcomed his suggestions. Besides, this was his territory. Unluckily, we sat there for about twenty minutes without so much as seeing a fish flash.

"Let's get out of here." Moondog primed the motor and gave it a pull. "Reel in and we'll go up a bit." James and I reeled in and stowed the rods as Moondog opened the throttle and kept to the river's center, away from the vegetation that spread into the water. The river became narrower and narrower, until finally the crowns of trees formed a seamless canopy overhead. We came to a deep backwater where Moondog cut the motor and we drifted into the tall grass. He took out an oar and felt for bottom. When he didn't find it, he gathered several blades of the tall grass into his hands and, pulling, used them to reposition the boat.

"Plants aren't the only problem, though: Got mongoose, goats, brown tree snakes, wild cats, and mountain pigs, a regular hodge-podge of destruction." As Moondog's list grew, the more dramatic and affected his voice became. Thinking he was joking, I laughed a little. "What's funny?" Moondog's eyes were a light, bluish-green and appeared much younger than the rest of his face. I looked away to sever the gaze and to find an answer: "Mountain pig sounded kinda funny." His mouth tightened and he raised his chin, but before he could say anything I asked what was being done about all these unwelcome guests.

"Give me a second," he said, turning to James. "Let me tie on something else for you, James. Frog seems to have lost its deadly . . . if it ever had it." What I thought was a rise a few yards up and against the bank turned out to be droppings from a bird that preened in the branches. Rise or no rise, I cast along the bank. I watched Moondog snip off the frog and hand James a bright yellow and green minnow. "This has Peacock written all over it." The sun fell in shafts and I could feel one burning my forearm. My line looked bowed so I started reeling in and the bow got smaller and smaller. "Damn," I said. "I got bottom." I was embarrassed by my inattention and complacency, but at the same time I was beginning to doubt that Moondog had actually put us on to some fish. He leaned over the gunwale and studied the problem.

"Maybe, but river bottoms usually don't move." He was right, my line was moving slightly downriver. I concentrated on the connection, trying to detect even the subtlest indicator of life. "I don't know," I said, holding the rod tip high. "Feels more like a log to me. You feel." I handed the rod to James for his opinion and he shrugged his shoulders and gave it back. "Then snap it off," Moondog said resignedly. "Either way, that tackle isn't going to raise what's down there. Hell, I'm not sure we'd want it to." I was curious, but I felt an even greater need to disconnect from whatever was working its way down to the ocean. I lowered the rod tip so it was flush with the line. I pulled slowly and something slowly pulled back until the line popped free.

"Depends on the animal," Moondog said, apparently in reference to my earlier question. "During fruiting season the ferals come down to feed and that's the best time and place to get them." Moondog searched his tackle box and produced a silver, purple, and yellow minnow that dangled three treble hooks. "Hand me your line," he said. I reeled in and pointed the rod so he could grab the line. "Ferals?" I asked. "Yeah, you know, the mountain boars you found amusing." He used his front teeth to clip the knot tail and then threw the minnow into the water. "Oh, right," I said.

"So you shoot them when they eat the fruit?" James asked. "You can, but I use a Bowie." Moondog made a clicking sound with his tongue and winked at James. "It's interesting that way." James soughed air through his nose and nodded in agreement. "In what sense?" I asked. Moondog unsheathed the knife on his hip—not his fabled Bowie—and patted his palm with the blade. "All of them. When you use a knife, you kill the pig with your whole body. The responsibility is 98% yours, give or take, depending on the size of the knife and how you use it. There's nothing like it."

Things were getting a little weird, so I tried to dilute the tension by asking James if he had on a fish. But Moondog was midstream. "You got to corner and grab him by his hinds before he turns on you." Moondog spat into the water and turned to James. "Do you got something on?" I think James was puzzled by all the interest. "Nope," he said, and then cast across the river. Moondog sat quietly for a couple minutes and watched us cast. I was beginning to think we had paid him $200 to fish dead water.

"So then what?" James asked, checking his back cast. "Pigwise?" Moondog asked coyly. "Yeah," James nodded. Moondog took a deep breath. "Cut the tendons right here so the pig can't run," he said, tracing his fingers along his Achilles heel. "Then I put him in a head lock and stab under the arm pit, hit the heart." He cracked a Shasta and drank. "If that doesn't do it right away, I cut his throat and bleed him out." I looked at the sun. "Sounds brutal," I mused. Moondog crushed his can and returned it to the cooler. "Killing usually is. But the meat is as good as any, and the island benefits. We've got a god damn invasion on our hands."

I could tell I had irritated Moondog by his tone, so before things could go any further south I said something stupid like *you've got to do what you've got to do.* What I should have said is that feral pigs don't have anything on humans when it comes to invasiveness. But as long as we were in his boat, I tried to keep it friendly. "You're right," he said. "Only difference

I see between me and other folks is I get a little face time with my food."
I nodded and scanned the water. A small feeder stream fringed with long
grass emptied into the river. I smiled when I realized that I was looking for
places where trout would hold. I couldn't bear the self-deception of fishing for trout in a place where trout don't exist, so I watched James—a bass
master in the making—and tried to pick up some pointers.

Moondog had since put on a straw hat. He looked at James, who hadn't
said more than handful of words all morning. "What do you think about
all this?" James cleaned some grass from his minnow and then leaned his
rod against the gunwale. "Think I could get one of those sodas?" Moondog dug a soda from the cooler and tossed it to him. James cracked it,
drank, and then belched politely under his breath. "I think I'd shoot 'em.
That way I wouldn't have to get their stink on me," he laughed. Moondog
shifted in his seat. "You have a point. No question, pigs are dirty animals."
He took off his hat, submerged it in the river, and then put it back on his
head. The water streamed down his face and neck. "But the fact doesn't
change. Put a plaid suit or a tutu on a dog and it's still a dog. A knife isn't
a gun isn't a spring trap or whatever method one uses to realize his willingness to kill. But the *will* is the same and comes from the killing place inside
each one of us."

"Whoa, shit!" James' rod tip bounced violently. "Set the hook, man"
Moondog yelled. "There we go," James said, holding the rod straight up.
"He's on." I sat up looking over the gunwale and saw a bright flash of
orange. "Is that a peacock?" "Sure is, and a nice one, too," Moondog said.
"Nicely done, James. But don't let him get under the boat. He'll do the
old wrap-around and that will be that." James held the rod away from the
boat while the fish pulled. "He nailed that minnow. Boom boom boom.
Just slammed it," James said excitedly. We had drifted out to the edge of
a sunspot and whenever the peacock swam there the river would ignite.
"Bring him around and I'll net him." Moondog stood at the ready and

when James finally lifted the bass from the darkness, he scooped up the fish and held him in the air, where it gaped and thrashed like a defiant offering to the sun.

That night I couldn't sleep so I got up and pulled on a pair of shorts and a T-shirt. As I turned to go, Kim asked what I was doing. "I'm going for a little walk. Go back to sleep." "OK," she said. "Be safe." I stood there for a moment and took in the details: The room was bathed in an opalescent blue light that I had not seen before and that I have not seen since. Kim was lying on her side beneath a sheet. I traced the outline of her body, which rose, fell, and rose before terminating in a sun-browned foot. The curtains moved like blue smoke and outside I could hear the surf breaking and the breezes hissing in the palm fronds. The scene of repose was such a stark contrast from everything I had seen earlier in the day and from what I imagined was going on just outside these walls. "Be back in a bit," I said, rubbing her foot, which was smooth and cool as a seashell.

I followed the path down to the beach and then strolled toward the cliffs where I had seen the man catch the yellow fin. The tide was in and the beach had been reduced to a berm of lion-colored sand. There was no moon but the edge of the surf glowed as it tumbled up the beach and withdrew into the heaving blackness. Now and then I would catch sight of a marauding crab picking its way along the beach, hunting the silver froth. I sat down and dug my heels into the sand. I looked out into the Pacific and was met by darkness so complete, when I closed my eyes it made no difference. The longer I sat there, the more it seemed I was losing my body and the ability to sense the world outside it. But it wasn't just the darkness: breezes neither hot nor cold, white noise of the surf, the faint smell of salt. Nothing to press against or to resist save for the ocean sucking the still-warm sand from beneath my feet, drawing all things forward into the water of the indifferent and devouring whole.

The Purist

Years ago I attended a party at a colleague's house to celebrate the beginning of fall semester. I had just relocated to Utah and thought it wise to get to know my colleagues, including our host. I wasn't fond of Rosley, but I respected him, both as a classic scholar and as someone who had survived the long and demanding life of an academic. How had he endured what the poet Theodore Roethke described as the dolor of pencils? The short answer, I'm convinced, is he fly fished. I had just started fly fishing myself three years before and, like any newcomer, I was beside myself. For whatever reason—perhaps because he had fished his entire life or that he was getting on in years—Rosley was rather sedate and a bit haughty. Despite these characteristics, I wondered what fishy wisdom the depths of this old water would reveal. We were colleagues, after all, so maybe he'd invite me to go fishing and share some of his hard-earned knowledge.

On some level, though, I knew I was being naïve. Even if he didn't just prefer to fish alone, it was likely he was selective when it came to fishing partners: They have a certain understanding that enables them to fish together unperturbed. Fundamentally, fly fishing with another person is a little like fishing with a detached shadow. This is not to say that partners, however similar, do not learn from each other nor bring novelty to the experience. It just means that if I'm standing riverside admiring a nice run or listening to the mating song of a yellow warbler, I'm not going to look over and see my partner pissing in the water or throwing his candy wrapper on the ground or whatever. Partners know the rules, not because they have been stated, but because individual philosophy has made contrary behavior virtually impossible.

In fairness to my former colleague, then, my own puerile optimism was partly to blame for our failure to connect. I had no reason to expect him to invite me to share something as personal as a day on the river. Although we never did fish together, we still exchanged what I think of now as tokens of our stations in life. At that time I nymphed probably ninety percent of the time and cast dry flies the rest. The same ratio described my tying habits as well. I had been experimenting with different bead head nymphs that I tied with a fine chamois and (perhaps in anticipation of my own maturation) silver, hair-thin wire. Sometimes I added a hackle to imitate the tiny legs of an emerger, but generally I left out the hackle to better emphasize the meaty, grub-like body of the nymph. This nymph and several variations were quite popular on the local rivers, especially the middle Provo, which is where many anglers I knew were fishing in order to avoid the crowded, lower Provo.

Assuming Rosley was among this group of migrants, I stopped by his office to offer him a half-dozen of my nymphs. His door was part way open and he was sitting at his computer with a book in his lap, looking over his glasses at the computer screen. "Knock, knock" I said. In his typical, detached fashion, Rosley didn't respond immediately, but instead he lingered on his work for a long and uncomfortable five seconds. As I turned to go he spun around in his chair, sat very erect, wiggled his head and said, "Yes, what is it?" That was the first time I realized Rosley and I could never fish together. He seemed too entrenched and unwilling to abandon the power structure that separates colleague from colleague. Out on the water, the power structure doesn't dissolve, exactly, but it is absorbed by the amplitude that is the experience of fly fishing. Therein lies the rub: Fly fishing is a social leveler, which can pose a problem for those who do not wish to be level.

"I thought you might enjoy these," I said, holding out my hand. Rosley's chair was on wheels, so instead of standing, he used his feet to roll to the middle of the floor. "Hmmmm," he said, peering down through his glasses, a hand on each knee. "Very nice of you, but I don't nymph." Obviously his refusal to accept the nymphs was mildly bad mannered, but I didn't give it much thought: Didn't nymph? What, you don't eat bread and butter? Nor did he fish streamers. Rosley was a bona fide, exclusive dry fly angler. The first so-called purist I'd ever met. And the only place he fished was on his own private stretch of the Logan River. "Well, in that case, let me give you a Deputy," I said in a last ditch attempt to rescue the moment from complete awkwardness. The Deputy was short for "Deputy of Darkness," which is a phrase I had taken from Cormac McCarthy's book *Blood Meridian*. But he didn't ask for the story behind the name and I didn't offer it. "All right, I'll give it a try."

I ran into Rosley a week later and asked how the fly had performed. "It caught a fish . . ." he said flatly. Before I could say anything, however, he added ". . . on the retrieve." Catching a trout while retrieving a dry fly is like catching a trout on a small streamer or an emerging nymph. In both cases the fly is wet, which could only mean one thing: The purist had been compromised. I wanted to ask him if he had bathed in the river afterward. "Well, I guess that's something," I said. That was the last time I saw Rosley, which was fine with me. I had learned all I was going to learn from him, which boiled down to three things: First, that some anglers sincerely believe they are purists; second, that purism, although it exists as a word, has no true counterpart in reality so far as anglers are concerned; and third, that while the enthusiasm we anglers have for fly fishing is a powerful and curious adhesive, that does not mean for one second that we are going to automatically like one another.

The notion that anglers are united in some special way, one that transcends human nature, is probably related to the idea that fly fishing and religion draw their essence from the same well. The comparison reminds me of the final moments of Hemingway's *The Sun Also Rises*. Jake—the impotent protagonist—and Brett—the unattainable embodiment of all his desire—are riding in a taxi:

"Oh, Jake," Brett said, "we could have had such a damned good time together."

"Yes," I said. "Isn't it pretty to think so?"

I know well the temptation to conflate the wonder inspired by the natural world with religious experience, but (and with all due respect to the Reverend Macleans of the world) if the purpose of comparison is to improve understanding, I wonder if it makes sense to equate fly fishing with religion. If I wish to gain insight into the distinctness of an Appaloosa relative to its original environment, I ought not to study unicorns. If, however, I look at the horses of Tibet and ask how their short legs and stout bodies might be the result of their mountainous environment, I may then come to better understand the uniqueness of the Appaloosa relative to its native home.

A cursory comparison between the Apache Trout (*Onchorhynchus apache*), which originated in the high deserts of Arizona, and the Rainbow Trout (*Onchorhynchus mykiss*) would suggest that their forms and habits are directly linked to their respective geographical and aquatic environments. Insofar as the apache is geographically isolated, its coloration does not significantly vary. But the rainbow's range extends from Mexico to Alaska and British Columbia, in which case its coloration is correspondingly varied and nuanced. Also, that the apache originated in slower water is suggested by its square caudal fin and compressed keel, whereas the rainbow's caudal fin is smaller, notched, torpedo-shaped, and thus adapted to moving water or currents that require greater navigability. I'm guessing a comparison of teeth would be equally insightful.

In the end, each angler must determine the veracity and usefulness of such comparisons and whether the beliefs that inform them are worth the expense. Ultimately, whether an angler displays the Jesus Fish or the Darwin Fish on the back of his fishmobile, the question is the same: In what ways do our ideas about ourselves and the world we inhabit help us to live and, when the time comes, to die? Maybe I'm asking too much. Perhaps the power of fly fishing (and the comparisons it invites) lies not in its confrontation with meaning, but in its escape from it. Pretty to think so.

Anglers' Ball

For Metcalf

When my children were in the first water of the womb, Kim and I would periodically eavesdrop on them with the ultrasound. I remember the tiny sprigs that would become hands and feet, the cartoonish skulls, the seahorse shaped bodies. And in the midst of it all was a crisp dash of blinking light, the electrical beating of their fierce and infinitesimal hearts. This flash of light pulses deep within living things, and so even when death finally alights it must insinuate itself, like a thief picking its way into the locked rooms of the body, until finally it reaches the last place, which, though diminutive, contains just enough light to write a letter by, enough to lead us out of the now darkened house and along the moonless lakeshore. My own death is calling to me, but the sounds of the river fill my ears so that I cannot hear it.

Last summer I invited death to go fishing on the Weber River. On the way there we listened to Morning Edition on NPR. The stories were sadly familiar: A suicide bomber killed himself and forty other men, women, and children in a market in Baghdad; two American soldiers were killed by a roadside bomb that had been stuffed into the chest of a dead dog; the body of a missing college girl was found inside her car in a river near her home town. "That's a fine trout river," death says. "World class." Then he takes a bite of muffin and chases it with a gulp of coffee. On this particular morning, northbound on Interstate 15, death is visiting my friend Jeff Metcalf, feeling him out, trying to read his light level. Too much light, death will hit the road; too little is an invitation to lay out the bedroll. I turned off the radio. "Had your fill?" Metcalf asks. I could see barn swallows feeding above the apple orchards. "My fill?" Jeff nods and offers me a thermos top of coffee. "Yeah," he says, his thick beard hiding his mouth. I shoot the coffee and then hand back the top. "Will things change if I say I have?"

When we get to the river, I turn onto a tractor road and park above the water. "Damn," I say. "Flows are way down." Metcalf leans over and looks out the window. "It does look low. Maybe 60 cfs?" I open the door, step out, and stretch. "Something like that. Lower than I've ever seen it." Although I'm soon busy rigging up, I'm still mindful of Metcalf. I note the six-foot, 3-weight Winston rod; the oversized duffle bags whose contents to this day remain a mystery; and at the end of it all, a squiggly, three-foot spike of line that resembles a pig's tail tied with a single fly. "What do you have in there?" I ask as Metcalf rummages through the back of his vest. "What I have in there, Maxee boy, is lunch. Take this," he says, tossing me what must be just under a pound of sandwich expertly wrapped in tin foil. "I can tell this ain't P B and J." Metcalf looks at me hard, as if I have committed a sacrilege. Then I smile and that does the trick. "Ohhhhoooo, no, no, no, no, my brother," he says, holding aloft his sandwich. "This is pesto, and Parma prosciutto, melted parmesan, and sautéed peppers on toasted Panini with a drizzle of hundred-year-old balsamic vinegar." He says all this as if it were an Italian melody, as if he tasted the words, their alternately sweet and salty music. I drop the sandwich into the back of my vest. I say *thank you* but I'm thinking *How can this be, Metcalf? How can you be so goddamn beautiful and alive and still be dying before my very eyes?*

We walk above the river, careful to avoid a remnant braid of barbed wire that weaves in and out of the tall yellow grass. I need some contrast so I look down through the vegetation and glimpse the sun on the Weber. In the low light of morning, the water appears milky and slightly golden. For a moment I am awash in happiness. I debate whether to say anything to Metcalf. Somehow it seems callous to remind him of how beautiful the world is now that he is preparing to leave it. I decide to merely point to the river and say "Look."

When Metcalf doesn't respond, I figure he has stopped to admire the golden water. "I knew you'd like . . ." I say, turning back. But Metcalf is not there. I scan the river and see him through the trees, *fishing* the milky strand of water. He looks up at me and I wave: "You're way ahead of me, man." He smiles and puts his left hand to his ear. I shake my head and wave *nothing*. Metcalf nods and gets back to work. Watching him down there with that six-foot rod, working maybe ten feet of water, his body leaning toward the river with each cast, head slightly tilted, as if he were both looking and listening: I realized how intimate fly fishing can be, how immediate and near. And how often times the farther I cast, the further away I get from myself and from the intensity of the moment.

That's the trouble with moments—there are only so many of them. I also sometimes find that those moments already lived are still alive, or would like to be. And that is why we experience the passage of time. Snow can fall on a mountain stream and evoke a feeling whose age cannot be known. This is one difference between memory and nostalgia. Nostalgia is generally painful because it is often without a precise referent. It is like autumnal air and autumnal light. Wind blowing dry red leaves into the streets. Which is why I feel grateful when I reach that place where the Weber narrows and slows along its southern bank. There I remember the exhilaration of catching a big rising brown some fifteen summers ago. Perhaps death is light receding, and the past is a faint glow that travels however far and lights the present moment. This is what I find each time I come to the Weber, or to any river with which I share a history.

As Metcalf works his line, I walk a few yards along the path and gaze up river. The trees on either side are thick with morning mist and birdsong. I have walked this path over a hundred times, alone and with friends, many of whom are now gone. Not *dead* gone, but gone just the same. When I get to be as old as Metcalf, *gone* will assume new meanings, and most will be final. I ought to thank the river. I ought to thank Metcalf and my other older friends for showing me how life changes as it starts to wind down. I can't see much of the future when I look at the friends my age. But with Metcalf, I see myself in twenty years. And so I prepare and I plan. It is a strange day. The sky is starting to cloud up and I can't shake the idea that whatever animates Metcalf is slowly leaving him. A few caddis flies appear above the water. One alights on my thumb, crawls to my wrist, and then flies away.

One summer evening I witnessed a full-fledged hatch, the likes of which I have not seen since. My friends Tae and Nole and I had fished until near dark and we were walking off the river when it began. Thousands of caddis flies filled the river corridor and rose some twenty feet into the air before they began to dissipate. They sheltered in my cuffs and crawled between the buttons of my shirt. I had a caddis in each nostril. "Better close your mouths," Tae said, laughing. *Or open them,* I thought, fantasizing that these were all the words I had ever spoken coming back to me. I remember looking down at the river and seeing the rolling silver and slashing fins of the fish as they gorged themselves. It didn't even occur to me to fish. Instead I stood there and witnessed the primordial spectacle of killing and eating.

Metcalf had since reeled in. "How did it go down there?" I ask him, extending a hand to help him step out of the river. He waves me off, kicks his toe into the bank, grabs a handful of grass, and hoists himself up. We make our way up river to a long run that has produced some big browns over the years. When we get there I'm tempted to tell him how I fish the hole, but I don't because I know he sees everything I do and more. He frees his fly and starts working his line out into the water. I happily give him the entire run, both because he is my guest and because I just happen to have the address of a large and wily trout just around the bend. A light rain starts to fall as I cross the river and make my way to the deep house, as I call it. Traversing the Weber can be tricky in high water, but with the low flows I make short work of it and am soon standing on the bottom of the deep run.

I cross to the other side and sit on the bank with my feet in the water. I know I miss too much when I'm fishing, so while the run is resting I take a few moments to notice my surroundings. Today's anglers can afford to have river vision, but I seriously doubt our early counterparts could give all their attention to a tiny dry fly riding atop the water. Rivers are resource-rich, and as such they would have attracted all manner of animals, many of which could kill an angler. Nowadays these threats have been largely eradicated from most of North America. Anglers can keep their backs to the woods for hours at a time without once turning around or looking over their shoulders. This is not to say that we don't still feel the need from time to time.

I can't see Metcalf, but I can hear him crossing down river. I move my foot a little and the water striders—also known as Jesus Bugs because they walk on water—scatter on either side of me. The run has been resting now for about five minutes. Waiting five minutes to angle for a huge trout is one of the hardest things I have ever done; third only to quitting smoking and walking off the beautiful Fremont River in southern Utah. But I do the unthinkable and I wait another sixty seconds just for good measure. Then I stand and free my nymphs. Rather then alternately stripping and paying out line, I bank about fifteen feet in preparation for a roll cast. I can feel the line as it slips cool and wet through my fingers. I roll my bugs into the headwater and watch for drag. I'm twelve feet away from the hole, and with only a slight difference between the speed of the run and the water around it, I don't have to do much. The river funnels into a trough against the bank, so all I do is roll my flies to the top of the run and let the river do its thing.

Within the last hour the water has cleared to a dark tea color. Earl Grey with a drop of cream. I still can't see the river bottom, however, which is fine because it probably means that the trout down there can't see me, either. I can think of a couple things I watch as closely as my strike indicator, and they have absolutely nothing to do with fly fishing. The moment it dips out of sight, I've already set the hook and I know instantly that the resident brown, the fella I came to see, has answered the dinner bell. I'm using Kim's rod, a locally made 6-weight, two-piece Snow. I used to have one exactly like it, but it inexplicably shattered when I was trying to free a snagged fly. I loved that rod. Now I'm loving Kim's as it does a fine job of balancing the trout's power and my experience of it, which seems to me now a kind of vampirism. But today I do not want the trout's blood. Instead I feed on his energy, his life force, his pulsing dash of light.

Weber River browns are surprisingly hearty for animals that must endure the noise pollution of regularly passing trains, as well as the chemical pollution from the cattle ranches that line the river. When I finally bring him to hand, I find the lord of the pool is no exception. I lay him down my forearm to establish his length. Just over eighteen inches and as round as a coffee mug. We look at each other for a moment, perhaps remembering, and then I return him to the river. He starts off slowly, and then bolts right back to where I found him and where—if he doesn't get wise, caught, or ousted—I will find him again. I notice my heart beginning to slow. Now that the rush of the fight is wearing off, I feel a little depleted, as the trout surely must.

For the moment, we are both emptied. But with no blood spilled the circle is left open and we live into its improbable space. I have no problem taking a trout from time to time. If I get a hankering for trout flesh, I could find the most beautiful trout on the end of my line and I would still kill it, lickety-split. No second thoughts. I'm not saying killing a trout is easy, however. The last trout I killed, I took from this very spot. Before then, I hadn't killed a trout for years, so I was unprepared for the sweet and sickening heat that washes over me whenever I hold that animal in my hands and take its life. Killing is not remembering, not quite forgetting, either. I know I have a killing-self that is contained by whatever else I am. My body is its camouflage. But some things cannot be hidden. Once the decision has been made, the killing-self does not judge or moralize: Impersonal, it steps forward and does what must be done. The dirty work.

One would not think that self-awareness could emerge in the throes of such abandon, but I remember moments when I would look up from my work and scan my surroundings. I am not sure why. I was within my rights to take as many as three trout if I had so chosen. Perhaps, because I was no longer concealed, I was afraid of what someone watching me would see—the ancient and artless me. Me hunched over this animal, grunting and cursing as I broke its head on a rock three or four times, once for each wave of nerves. Once was enough, of course, but I panicked. When the trout finally stilled, I laid him in a small pool someone had built with a ring of rocks. Then I tried to calm down. My hands felt plump with blood and were glistening with trout sheen and river water. I stood there beneath the rain-black clouds, a mindless and sweat-soaked killer. A swirl of yellow line uncurls across the water and returns me to the here and now. I walk a few feet down the bank and call to Metcalf: "How are you doing?" The question hadn't left my mouth and I was cursing myself for not asking a better one.

When Metcalf's line reaches the bottom of the run, he rolls it to the top with the flick of his wrist, mends it, and calls back: "I'm coming up." I nod and take a seat on the bank. *Serves you right*, I say to myself. *Next time you see a burning house, why not just ask the man standing in the middle of it how he's doing?* I shake my head and spit in the water. A couple feet away from me, the Jesus Bugs have congregated around a moth that has fallen into the water. They seem to avoid the wings and instead focus on the supple abdomen. Above me a pair of Warbling Vireos hunt the leaves for insects. And cancer cells raft the blood streams of the body. Eventually they haul out and grow like black grass along the banks. The rain stops and in the ensuing quiet I imagine rising into the stratosphere, where I settle in for a good, long listen to the Earth. I close my eyes and I hear what I suspect is the far-off sound of burning. But deep down I know fire makes us all fools. What I am really hearing is the sound of chewing.

I can't stand deception. It's hard, though, because I want to say something helpful to Metcalf. I want to reassure him in some absolute way. But I can't make any promises, so instead I pat him on the back. I note the thickness of his skin and muscle. Despite the chemo, there's still a lot to him. He doesn't *look* like someone with cancer. The rain is falling again but I can still feel the sun. I look at Metcalf and the sun is on his face. "It's good to be here with you," I tell him. He drinks some water. "You too, man. This is a beautiful place." He tips his bottle of water in a kind of toast: "Trout live in beautiful places." I raise my water: "Cheers. What happened down there?" Metcalf looks down river and then back at me. "What *didn't* happen down there?" he laughs. I laugh, too, because Metcalf has a silly grin on his face. Despite our twenty-year age difference, had we grown up together as children, I am certain we would have palled around. "Touch any fish?" he asks, taking out a sandwich. "I just put back an eighteen-incher I coaxed out of there," I say, nodding toward the trough. Metcalf was about to respond when a train approached from up the canyon. The tracks are just across the river, maybe fifty feet away. I could just barely make out the dark outline of the engineer before the train sped past.

The train gone, Metcalf looks at the trough and smiles. "The trout are right where they should be." When it comes to fly fishing, or anything else, for that matter, Metcalf is not the kind of guy I like to contradict, but claims of what "should be" make me uncomfortable. "Maybe so," I muse. "But sometimes they are where they should not be." I don't believe a word I just said, of course. Trout are where they are. Whether they should or should not be there is sort of beside the point. Metcalf doesn't miss a beat: "You're a real smart ass, you know that?" I'm a little embarrassed, but I muster, "I guess that's better than the alternative." Metcalf smiles and shakes his head. Then he takes a bite of his sandwich and closes his eyes. I know this is a private moment, but I don't turn away. Instead I note the calmness of Metcalf's face, the neatly trimmed beard, and nostrils expanding and relaxing. And outside both our lives, the river and the day go by. He chews slowly, lovingly, his jaws working as he enjoys the richness of the flavors; perhaps remembering the slow burn of the moment—savoring its sweetness, bitterness, and everything else it is—while it lasts.

The Afterglow

A year after my parents called it quits and my mother, siblings, and I moved out West, my father flew us kids back east to spend the summer with him on Peaks Island, which is just off the coast of southern Maine. The house he had rented there wasn't much but it kept out the rain and was built in a forest of pines we could wander in the off hours. The pines were so dense it seemed like evening all the time, as though the house and everything in it had absorbed the shadows. We left open the windows and lit incense but could not kill the musty odor of damp furniture, wood rot, and my father's running shoes. Some nights the fog would roll in as if it owned the place and we would watch it settle on the floor. If the house were not a short walk from Josiah's Cove, where we spent our days braving the frigid Atlantic and drying in the August sun, we would have committed island mutiny.

Beyond the cove the open ocean was spotted with lobster buoys and fishing trawlers that would disappear into the horizon. As a twelve-year-old, I did not realize they fished for days and miles out to sea. As the sun went down I would shield my eyes, scan the darkening horizon, and wonder why none were coming back. In the evenings we would ride our bikes to Trefethen Landing and watch the locals and the lights come on across the bay. Young men in jeans did swan dives from the ferry moorings while the girls smoked and gossiped. I was curious about the diving, but I was more interested in the man who came down to the landing each dusk to fish for mackerel.

A skinny marmalade cat sat next to the man and would often swoon his boots and meow but no sound would come out. The stink of bait made me dizzy and spiked the melded sweetness of pipe smoke, soap, and the oddly pleasing smell of oil that preserved the pier timbers. Among the man's personals was a saltwater fly rod tied with a minnow made of clean white rabbit fur, red eyes, and a large silver hook that peeked out of the fur. I never did see him fish the rod, and I wonder now if he were waiting for the right time to use it.

So maybe some night just as a storm is coming in, the man's wife appears in her nightgown at the end of the pier. She is the age she was when they first met and he knows she isn't really there because her nightgown is dripping stars. After she hands him the rod, she stands behind him and helps him with the motion. The line spools out like light, connecting them to the dark water. At her suggestion, the man strips in the line. He doesn't care about any of it because he is with her. He is therefore unprepared when the fish takes his bait. Then he wishes it hadn't. The fish is stronger than anything he has known. *Either let go or be taken.* "Let go" his wife says just outside the wilted flower of his ear. "I can't." She has been holding him until now. "Go ahead. It's OK." But he can see the fish swirling beneath the water. "It's not." A moment later they are both gone and sand from his shoes blows across the pier.

Another possibility is that he liked to preserve things for as long as he could. Whatever the reason, when the man checked his hook I would gaze down at the hull of a trawler that lay submerged against the pilings. The surf would roll through that corroded mansion for sea life, including large crabs whose carapaces gleamed up at me like blank faces. I listened to the surf with one ear and with the other I waited for the prayer the man would mumble before each cast. I would watch him until he was nothing but coughs and pipe-flare. Once I heard a mackerel flopping on the pier, and a faint squeal, like seeps of air escaping from a party balloon. Luckily for anglers, fish don't pray.

My father saw the man catching fish and the birds in his head started flying. Inspired, he took the rod and tackle that belonged to the house and rode an old ten-speed down to the landing in his shorts and shirtsleeves. If each person could be a thousand things, one of the last my father would be is a fisherman. Despite the fact, he showed up with the moon and the stars and ingredients for a late dinner. The fish was stiff and the color of unpolished silver. "Don't be fooled by the appearance," he winced as the fish's inner life spilled over his knuckles. I would have shared my father's philosophy had the mackerel tasted as beautiful as the ocean that had grown it. Maybe the meat was awash with adrenaline from a bad killing or my father simply added too much soy. Regardless, two-thirds of the dish—a mixture of brown rice, fish, and scallions—fed the woods. The raccoons were pleased. I heard them squabble as my father sat and ate with our empty chairs and full bowls.

Nights on the island were dark and secular. The new bed slept as if it were stuffed with fallen leaves, but after about a week I had accepted its strangeness and was lulled by the sound of the fog horn. By the time we left the island, I wondered how I was going to fall asleep without that long low tuba note blowing out there in the night. I needed the lullaby because in the wee hours big storms would blow in from the North Atlantic. If not for the wreckage of the next day those storms would have remained those of my dreams. The ocean put ashore drift nets, swaths of seaweed, and lobster traps. We had met two brothers, year-rounders who, privy to such windfall, would rise before dawn and comb the shore in search of treasures. By sunup the wind had calmed to a breeze and I would see them toting booty in canvas bags. One morning the older brother stopped by the house. His hair was like salted straw and he wore the remnants of sunburn and an extra-large tank top that hung like a dress. He set down his bag and opened it.

Inside was a raw stew of pungent seaweed, bottles, cans, and a piece of driftwood shaped like an umbrella. "So?" The boy stooped and placed his hands into the bag, dug around, and then withdrew them. "Look now," he said, holding the bag just so. Down in the very bottom, kept cool by a thick bed of seaweed, were three lobsters he had stolen from beached traps. "Put your ear in the bag." I studied the boy's face to see if he had ill intentions and then I put my ear into the bag. I have always wondered what other animals were saying, but with those lobsters I already knew. Although I felt mild sympathy for them, I would have joyfully devoured their sweet flesh. After the hunger surge had passed, however, I was troubled by how easy it was to obtain this exquisite animal. I looked at the boy's shoes: He didn't even get his feet wet. In the short history of my life, almost nothing had been so easy.

That was a long time ago. Tonight I think of the man standing in match light, match hand trembling, body twisted into a painful question mark from sitting for who knows how long. In him I see that however much life may rise, roots grow down, and we know belonging by how far into the watery dark we are willing to go to find it.

Wolves, Grizzlies & Greenhorns

Death and Coexistence in the American West

By: Maximilian Werner
ISBN: 978-0-88839-537-5 [Trade Paperback]
ISBN: 978-0-88839-578-8 [eBook]
Binding: Trade Paper
Size: 5.5" X 8.5"
Pages: 352
Illustrations/Photos: 1
Publication Date: 01 May 2021

In *Wolves, Grizzlies, and Greenhorns -- Death and Coexistence in the American West*, Werner recounts the two-and-a-half years he spent tracking down and looking after a wolf pack that was rumored to have settled in the Centennial Valley of southwest Montana. Along the way he encounters and reflects on the lives of other animals, including deer, elk, fox, coyote, skunks, and grizzly bears. But he also encounters other humans too—ranchers, hunters, land and wildlife managers, cowboys—who offer their own, often conflicting perspectives about the natural world, other animals, and how both ought to be treated.

In the wild, wide-open landscapes of the American West, how animals are treated depends on the stories people tell about them, as well as on their ability to steer clear of humans and their livestock—no easy task for animals that are running out of places to go!

The story of conflict between humans and wildlife is as old as humanity. But the landscapes of today bear little resemblance to the landscapes of the past. Over the last several hundred years, human consumption, development, greed, and over-population have increasingly displaced large predators. We need new, more nuanced, compassionate, empathetic stories, Werner argues; stories that recognize our place within the natural order, and the value of wild places and other animals' right to live free of human interference. *Wolves, Grizzlies, and Greenhorns – Death and Coexistence in the American West* is one of those stories.

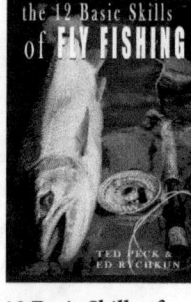

www.ingramcontent.com/pod-product-compliance
Lightning Source LLC
Chambersburg PA
CBHW051836020726
47502CB00005B/1814